Sundardas

Sundardas

A PLAY IN THREE ACTS

J.P. Das

Translated from the Oriya by

Paul St-Pierre

K K Mohapatra

Leelawati Mohapatra

NATIONAL SCHOOL OF DRAMA

in association with

HAR-ANAND PUBLICATIONS PVT LTD

HAR-ANAND PUBLICATIONS PVT LTD
D-9, Anand Niketan, New Delhi - 110 021
Tel.: 4101983, 4101962 Fax: 011-5121049
E-mail: haranand@mantraonline.com

PRINTED IN INDIA

Published by Ashok Gosain and Ashish Gosain for Har-Anand Publications Pvt Ltd and printed at Taj Press

Contents

Introduction

Sundardas recounts the activities of the first Christian missionaries in Orissa between 1826 and 1832, their meagre successes, their discouragement and defeats. But the play is more than a simple retelling of the historical facts; rather, it gives reality to the underlying motivations of the individual actors, as well as to the conflicting worldviews in contact in this meeting of Christianity and Hinduism on the Indian subcontinent, in a context of empire, subjugation and colonization.

But the real question dealt with in the play is a more philosophical one, that is, the nature of the relationship between belief and the (religious) institutions whose role ostensibly is to further and protect it. Through the focus on Sundardas the sage this question is played out, as he attempts to place himself outside and beyond all institutions but at the same time is constantly confronted with the limits they impose. Sundardas is a fundamentally iconoclastic figure, but one who, nevertheless, finds himself ensnared by the beliefs and expectations of others, those of his followers on the one hand and of the missionaries on the other. The former believe him to be a worker of miracles; they attach themselves to him and make him their guru. His relation to the missionaries is scarcely different, as they mistake his iconoclasm for a desire to convert and his interest in Christian texts for burgeoning belief. Their error arises out of their adherence to religion in its institutionalized form; for them, recognition of the truth contained within a particular text leads of necessity to the renunciation of former beliefs, now deemed false, and conversion to the new truth. But these expectations are based on a misunderstanding, for Sundardas, while rejecting rituals, caste, and other attributes of Hinduism, maintains steadfastedly that he nevertheless is, and will remain, a Hindu. Sundardas feels no need to turn from Hinduism to Christianity; his quest for truth locates him outside the institutions of either.

Sundardas underscores various paradoxes running through the lives of the different characters, most notably the conflicting values of the secular and the religious, syncretism versus separation. Such a conflict is found at the very heart of the colonial project. Thus despite their both being instruments of empire, the missionaries and the East India Company are constantly at loggerheads; the justice dispensed by the employees of the Company serving to marginalize all forms of religion. The missionaries, too, are caught up in this conflict, as they reproduce the very hierarchies they wish to subvert. Although they may preach to lower-caste villagers, the missionaries pay them little heed and focus their attention on the conversion of Brahmins. Nor is Sundardas himself untouched by the power of the constraints he is putting into question. Thus, while claiming to espouse the principle of equality between the sexes, he accords greater freedom of thought, of choice and of action to men.

The play illustrates the problematic nature of conversion, insofar as it implies the rejection of one's past and the adoption of a new identity. And here the figure of Balabhadra and his changing names—Balia in his village, Meria to the Kondhs, Balabhadra in Sundardas's ashram, and finally David in the mission—is significant. He can be at home nowhere, and is constantly on the verge of running away. The fundamental theme of the play—that truth can not come through the denial of one's identity, but also that identity must not blind one to truth—is crystallized in the central figure of Sundardas, as he attempts to negotiate the different relationships and social structures which envelop him. In the end his only recourse is to sink into a form of solipsistic madness.

Paul St-Pierre

Sundardas

Characters

Sundardas, a sadhu
William Bampton
Charles Lacey
Amos Sutton
Gangadhar Sarangi
Ramachandra Jachak
Marua—Mary
Balabhadra—David
Krupasindhu Sahu
Radhu Das
Raghu
Irun Senapati
Devika
Kamali
Daani
Brother Pears
Ann Lacey
Buda Munda
Ratana Pana
Ramachandra's Mother, Wife and Son
Husbands of Kamali and Daani
Disciples
Brahmins
Soldier
Fakir
Pundit
Madman
Villagers

ACT ONE

The ashram of SUNDARDAS, *a sadhu. A raised mud platform around a shady tree where people like to congregate. Morning.* SUNDARDAS*'s disciples,* GANGADHAR SARANGI, RAMACHANDRA JACHAK *and his wife* LAXMI, KRUPASINDHU SAHU*'s wife* DEVIKA *and some other women:* KAMALI, *her mother* DAANI *and* MARUA. *Also two Brahmins from a nearby village, and* BALABHADRA, *who narrowly escaped being made a meria (human sacrifice) by the hill people. All are waiting for* SUNDARDAS *to come out of his hut.* GANGADHAR *is busy writing something on a palm-leaf with a stylus, and* BALABHADRA *is trying to carry on a conversation with him.*

Scene I

GANGADHAR: Be quiet, will you, Balabhadra, my boy? Don't talk to me till I've finished writing. After that I'll be happy to listen to you for as long as you wish.

BALABHADRA: Carry on with your writing. I'd better be off.

GANGADHAR: (*Closes the palm-leaf scroll.*) Off where—back to the hills? Are you hoping to get caught by the tribesmen again and be sacrificed?

BALABHADRA: That wouldn't be so bad. Right up to the end you live a life of luxury. Nothing's denied you—delicacies of every kind, freedom to do whatever you want. You can walk into anyone's house, no doors are closed to you. But here, all the time it's do this, do that! From morning to night! So many rules: Bathe twice a day, don't eat fish or meat, don't chew tobacco, don't smoke. A thousand dos and don'ts.

GANGADHAR: Listen Balabhadra, this is an ashram and not some godforsaken hell-hole in the remote hills.

BRAHMIN I, *one of the two Brahmins who have been listening to the conversation, inches closer.*

BRAHMIN I: Just what sort of an ashram is this? There aren't any idols; there's no worship, no priests!

GANGADHAR: Not a typical one, certainly. The caste system isn't enforced. Baba says there are no castes, that all men are equal. Here you'll find Brahmins, Kshatriyas, Vaisyas and Sudras mingling freely and praying together.

BRAHMIN I: Go ahead and pray. By all means, pray. But where's the temple?

GANGADHAR: Baba says there's no need for temples or idols. Nor for fasts or vigils, rituals or pilgrimages. Holy ashes, marks on the forehead, sandalwood paste, the sacred thread and the water jug are only for show. True worship needs no pilgrimages, no cows, no Brahmins, no consecrated food, no idols, no images, whether made of stone or wood.

BRAHMIN II: What then does this Baba of yours preach?

GANGADHAR: That people should not tell lies, or discriminate on the basis of caste; that they should not take any life, whether human or animal; that they should not cut down trees or destroy forests, steal or commit adultery; that they should not give in to anger, jealousy or hatred.

BRAHMIN I: And you practise this?

GANGADHAR: Yes, this is what we try to practise. We take a morning bath. We don't eat fish or meat, chew tobacco or smoke. We don't tell lies or speak falsehoods. We don't steal, don't look upon women with lust, don't indulge in idol worship. We've uprooted all the basil plants in the courtyard and thrown them away. We don't go on pilgrimages. Fasts and vigils are things of the past. As are consecrated food, the company of the devil, Brahmins and priests.

BRAHMIN II: So this is what that Baba of yours has told you to do? Is this what your religion is about?

GANGADHAR: Baba says that God is everywhere; that we should not answer hate with hate or hit back; that it's wrong to cheat anyone; that we should love our enemies as much as our friends, and love our wife and children as much as we love ourself; that it is important to respect our parents and elders, and not to bear false witness; that we should have equal respect for all human beings, no matter what caste, and give alms to the poor. These are the articles of our faith and we try to practise them.

BRAHMIN I: What rubbish! Show me where in the scriptures all these things are mentioned.

GANGADHAR: What do you know about the scriptures? Come and listen to Baba speak if you want to learn about the scriptures.

BRAHMIN II: Listen here, we're Brahmins of the purest Kanyakubja stock; we arrived here at the time of King Janmejaya's great snake-sacrifice! We don't need riff-raff like you to lecture us about the scriptures. We know what abominable practices are being practised in this ashram. We know that you don't pay any heed to the sacred caste system, that you've been reading books printed on paper, that you're dabbling in Christian scriptures. You are the enemies of Hinduism. You'll be the ruin of our ancient religion. You've drawn not only men but women too to your vile ways.

MARUA *moves closer to the* BRAHMIN II.

MARUA: Repeat what you just said, thread-wearer.

BRAHMIN II: Keep away, woman. Don't you dare to come nearer. What are you up to—trying to pollute me this morning?

MARUA: Yes, trying to pollute you. How come you forget about it at night? Come morning caste seems to be uppermost in your mind once again. (*Turns to* KAMALI.) Kamali, isn't this the same Brahmin who runs after you too? No wonder these people can't stand Baba when he preaches equality between men and women.

BRAHMIN I: Woman, you've already lost your caste, so stop going on about it, will you?

MARUA: So according to you Brahmins, as a woman I'm untouchable, is that right? I don't belong anywhere, is that what you think?

BRAHMIN II: You know very well why you were thrown out of your caste.

MARUA: Just because I agreed to do the housework for a Firinghee? Why don't you treat all the Brahmins and Kshatriyas who've taken up work in Firinghee households as cooks, gardeners and torchbearers the same? Why don't you treat them all as outcastes? Just because I'm a poor woman with no one to defend me you're picking on me. Do you have so little shame that you even boast about it? But what more harm can you cause me? I'm better off now. My new home is better than those in the village.

BRAHMIN I: Better off? Why not! You've taken whatever tainted money from the Company came your way.

GANGADHAR: Brother, it's not for you to lecture us. Don't you know that your great Lord Jagannath Temple at Puri is being run with the tainted money of the Company?

MARUA: And don't forget who went to welcome the Company when it invaded Orissa! Who other than the good Brahmin priests and attendants from the holy temple?

BRAHMIN II: This woman has gone mad. That's what happens if you give women a little freedom.

MARUA: Women, women! Stop complaining about them, will you? Hey Laxmi, Devika, Daani, what are you waiting for? Come, give me a hand, help me throttle this lousy Brahmin. Kamali, come here, woman.

KAMALI *moves closer to* BRAHMIN II.

BRAHMIN II: (*Backs away.*) All right, all right. Let's have it out with your Sundara Baba once and for all; we've had enough. How long can we shut our eyes to the abominations going on here? Just exactly what does go on here day and night? Why are all these women hanging around?

KAMALI: But no problem that the men are, huh? Women should stay at home, is that right? Women, stay at home, cook, look after the babies, take care of the lord and master, keep the household running! Eat only crumbs and leftovers, swallow insults cheerfully, accept the slaps, kicks and blows gracefully; hide indoors, don't ever stay outside for a moment. (*Points to the Brahmins.*) Look how angry they're getting just because Sundara Baba treats men and women equal! That's what makes them see red, isn't it, Laxmi?

LAXMI: What more is there to say? Sundara Baba is like God to us. (*She crosses over to her husband,* RAMACHANDRA.) Could I have married this man without Baba's blessings? When my father fixed my marriage with somebody else for five *bharans* of paddy and fifty rupees I refused to be sold like cattle. (RAMACHANDRA *puts his arm around her protectively.*) It was Baba who saved me.

DEVIKA: Remember how I kept losing one child after another no sooner than they were born? The Brahmins hit upon the silly idea of taking me and my husband through the wedding rituals again, but that didn't help. It was only after we took refuge here in Baba's ashram that the problem ended. Our last three children have survived.

MARUA: Say what you will, but the Firinghees show respect to women. And it's the same way in Baba's ashram. Baba makes no difference between men and women.

BRAHMIN I: I'm waiting for your Baba to come out of his hut. I can't wait to give him a piece of my mind.

BALABHADRA *goes inside and comes out carrying a bundle. Everyone falls silent. He walks up to* GANGADHAR.

BALABHADRA: I'm off. Tell Baba I couldn't stand this place any longer.

GANGADHAR: Boy, nobody invited you here in the first place. You came of your own accord, after narrowly escaping being sacrificed by the Kondhs. Nobody's forcing you to stay; you're free to leave.

MARUA: But where are you going to go? Six months in the ashram and you've completely forgotten your past. Some people have short memories! How can you say you were better off with the Kondhs? Didn't you realize they were fattening you up so that there would be enough flesh for everyone when you were sacrificed? You'd have been buried in their turmeric fields. Go, go back to the Kondhs. Go and eat to your fill and get fat and be sacrificed.

BALABHADRA *storms out, but returns immediately in great agitation.*

BALABHADRA: A white man's headed this way.
MARUA: Scared out of your wits, boy? Let the Firinghee come, he's not going to gobble you up.

Enter old padre BAMPTON, *dressed like a native in dhoti and vest. He is barefooted.*

BAMPTON: (*To himself.*) Where's my horse? Where's it gone? (*He looks around. The sight of a congregation gladdens his heart. He begins to preach with a song.*)

Who else other than
Our Lord Jesus Christ
Can save us
From this world of sin?
It's only He
The son of God
The only saviour!
He who prays to Him
Is redeemed.

My dear brothers and sisters! Have you any idea what brings me here?
MARUA: Your horse! (*Mimicks him.*) Where's my horse, where's it gone?
BAMPTON: So what if my horse isn't here? You good people are!
MARUA: You want to ride us or what?

BAMPTON: I'll show you the path to redemption. How to escape hell! Hell is all fire, brimstone and the stench of sulphur. The Holy Bible says all sinners are damned and human beings are sinful by nature. But there's still hope. Let me tell you about it. There's only one God and He loves us all.

MARUA: Loves only you Christians.

BAMPTON: He loves Hindus too. God has a Son and His name is Jesus Christ. Jesu Krista, you may call Him. Jesu Krista was originally with God the Father. But God the Father was so concerned about this sinful world of ours that He sacrificed His son. He who puts his faith in Him will not only be saved but will enjoy eternal life. Jesu Krista sacrificed His own life for our sins. If we put our trust in Him, His blood will save us from damnation. This is the secret of salvation. There is no other path to redemption. He's the only redeemer, there is no other. Amen. Bring my horse.

BAMPTON *takes out the watch tucked in at his waist and, singing 'Who else can save', hurries out as if he has just remembered that he should be somewhere else. A moment later he returns, takes a good look at the gathering and says to himself, 'No, my horse isn't here', and exits.*

MARUA: Of course your horse isn't here. There're only human beings here.

RAMACHANDRA: Who was that clown, Marua? Why's a Firinghee dressed so strangely?

MARUA: Surely you don't expect me to know all the Firinghees! That man spoke like a padre but wasn't dressed like one. He could be a padre gone mad. Whites too have their fair share of madmen. (*Mimicks.*) Bring my horse. Oh my!

BALABHADRA *looks around and finds* BAMPTON *gone.*

BALABHADRA: The fellow's nowhere to be seen.

GANGADHAR: Be off then, if you must.

BALABHADRA: I'd like to stay, but I feel very homesick.

GANGADHAR: Go home then.

BALABHADRA: On second thought, I won't go home. If my people could sell me to Death for a few rupees, why should I go back? I'll go somewhere else. Goodbye. Goodbye to you all. This time I'm really off.

MARUA: Goodbye, Moonface. Don't let the sight of a Firinghee scare you into scampering back.

BALABHADRA *leaves in a huff. The very next moment, he's back, shaking with fear. He has lost his bundle somewhere. He runs to* RAMACHANDRA *and clings to him.*

RAMACHANDRA: What's the matter now?

BALABHADRA: They're here, they're here! They're going to catch me again.

RAMACHANDRA: Who?

BALABHADRA: The Kondhs, the hill people.

Enter RATANA PANA *and* BUDA MUNDA. BALABHADRA *tries to hide.*

BUDA MUNDA: He made a fool of Buda Munda and escaped. The moment we were a little tipsy he slipped the chains off his hands and legs and ran away. But look, Ratana Pana, what did I tell you? Didn't I tell you I'd find him even if I had to go to the end of the earth?

RATANA PANA: See to it he doesn't give us the slip a second time.

BUDA MUNDA: This time I'll put the axe to his neck myself.

They move closer to catch hold of BALABHADRA.

GANGADHAR: Stop it! This is an ashram, for heaven's sake, not some godforsaken hole in the hills. None of your antics here!

BUDA MUNDA: Hand us over our meria and we'll be gone.

GANGADHAR *looks at* MARUA *playfully as if wondering if it wouldn't be a good idea to hand over* BALABHADRA *to the tribesmen.* MARUA *nods in assent.* BALABHADRA *joins his palms in supplication, pulls his own ears, indicating he'll never again talk of leaving the ashram.*

GANGADHAR: Look, these aren't the dark hills you people come from. Go away without causing trouble, or else we'll get the police to handcuff you and haul you off to jail.

The tribesmen pay no heed and chase BALABHADRA, *who ducks behind* BRAHMIN I *and pushes* BRAHMIN II *towards* BUDA MUNDA. *In his confusion,* BUDA MUNDA *grabs* BRAHMIN II, *but releases him immediately after realising his mistake.*

BRAHMIN II: (*Begins to howl.*) I've been sullied! I've been polluted! I've lost my caste!

The commotion takes some time to subside. SUNDARDAS *is seen standing on the platform. His head is shaved; he's old but full of energy. His face is creased in a smile.*

SUNDARDAS: There are a lot of visitors today. (*Looks around.*) Gangadhar, Ramachandra, Laxmi, Devika, Kamali, Daani, Marua, Balabhadra. Who're the new faces, Gangadhar?

GANGADHAR: (*Points out.*) These two Brahmins are from Chowdwar. They've come to engage you in a debate on the scriptures. (BHAHMIN I *and* BRAHMIN II *seem distinctly uncomfortable.*) And these two are from the hills.

SUNDARDAS: Very well. But why was there such a commotion a few moments ago?

GANGADHAR: The hill people want to take Balabhadra back with them.

SUNDARDAS: Very well.

BALABHADRA: Very well? Baba, they want to sacrifice me to their god.

SUNDARDAS: A human sacrifice? What do the scriptures have to say about that?

GANGADHAR: (*Looks at the Brahmins, who hang their heads.*) Satpath Brahman has references to animal sacrifice. But all it discusses is the distribution of the sacrificial meat.

SUNDARDAS: And on the subject of human sacrifice?

GANGADHAR: The Yajur Veda mentions human sacrifice. The relevant mantras are to be found in the Taittiriya Samhita. The ones indulging in it were the Brahmins and the Kshatriyas who wished to rise to greater heights.

SUNDARDAS: Is that what these men from the hills want – to rise to the top? (*Looks at* RATANA PANA *and* BUDA MUNDA.) What do they want?

GANGADHAR: They want to propitiate Mother Earth with a human sacrifice.

BUDA MUNDA: Enough discussion. Hand the boy over and then we'll leave. We paid good money for him.

SUNDARDAS: You bought a human being? What do the scriptures say about that, Gangadhar?

GANGADHAR: Aitareya Brahman has it that King Harischandra had promised to sacrifice his own son Rohit to Varun, the water-god. Rohit went around looking for someone to take his place and finally found a Brahmin named Ajigarta, who was willing to sell his second son Sunahsepa. Rohit bought him with a hundred cows.

SUNDARDAS: How awful! How unjust! Was Sunahsepa sacrificed?

GANGADHAR: No. The priests refused to tie him to the sacrificial stake.

SUNDARDAS: What happened then?

GANGADHAR: For another hundred cows Ajigarta himself tied his son to the stake. But the priests refused to put the knife to the boy's throat. The father was willing to do it himself for another hundred cows.

SUNDARDAS: So in the end it was the father who killed his own son?

GANGADHAR: Mercifully, no. Sunahsepa prayed to the Gods . . . Verse after verse, the cords that bound him came undone. He was freed.

SUNDARDAS: And father and son were reunited?

GANGADHAR: The boy refused to go back to his father. He said any father willing to kill his own son for three hundred cows did not deserve to have one.

SUNDARDAS: Greed and human sacrifice are equally abominable. (*Looks at* BUDA MUNDA *and* RATANA PANA.) Could you understand, even a little?

RATANA PANA: We don't have to. We paid twenty-five rupees to the father of this boy and saved him to be sacrificed. From time immemorial we have been offering human sacrifices to Mother Earth. If they stop, our god will become annoyed and our fields will turn barren. We've got to take back the meria.

SUNDARDAS: Anything in the scriptures in their favour, Gangadhar?

GANGADHAR: Kautilya talks of the practice of buying and selling bipeds. Any deceitful transaction had a penalty of twelve *pons*. If somebody lost a slave, he had to pay five *pons* to get him back. If somebody forcibly captured a temple slave he deserved the severest punishment. But there's no reference to human beings bought to be sacrificed who run away.

SUNDARDAS: What does the Book have to say about it?

GANGADHAR: In the Old Testament it just says: And he that stealth a man, and selleth him, or if he be found in his hand, he shall surely be put to death.

SUNDARDAS: (*Looks solemnly at* BUDA MUNDA *and* RATANA PANA) Capital punishment!

BUDA MUNDA: Capital punishment or whatever, but we refuse to budge without the boy. Without a sacrifice our lands will remain barren and there'll be a famine. You want us to die of starvation?

BRAHMIN I: Not only you, but everyone else will die. The Kaliyug isn't far off, considering how low we seem to have plunged.

SUNDARDAS: The Kaliyug? What will happen in the Kaliyug?

BRAHMIN II: There will be droughts, famines, natural calamities. There's a long chapter about it in the Bhagavat. (He and BRAHMIN I *start in a singsong voice, each quoting one line.*)
The rich will rule the earth.
Women will choose their partners.
Upstarts, proud wretches will be in power.
Virtuous men will be ignored.
Women will consort with their own kind
and men with men.
Whores will be more sought after than good women.
People will forsake their caste.
There will be free mingling of the castes
and ignoble paths will seem attractive.
Anarchy will rule.
The King of Gods will give no rains
and famines will visit the land.

SUNDARDAS: Did you hear that, children? There're famines in the offing.

BRAHMIN I: That's not all. (*Sings.*)
Righteousness of every kind shall vanish.
The tribe of criminals shall increase.
Rulers will turn robbers
and the ruled will revel
in thieving, lying, quarrelling and back-stabbing.
Even cows will become worse than goats
and eat whatever they never should
and their milk will turn into poison.
There will be no crops, nor anything else.
Pitiful rains and no cultivation.
Homes will be deserted
and men will take to begging
even as they toil like donkeys.
And like fish to water, women
will take to adultery.

RATANA PANA: Save your scriptures for later, and settle our problem first. We're in a hurry to get back home with our meria.

SUNDARDAS: Have something to eat first.

RAMACHANDRA *invites them to have something to eat, but they decline and do not move.*

SUNDARDAS: What a fine discussion on the Kaliyug, thanks to the ever so enlightened Brahmins of Chowdwar. But why should the Kaliyug be upon us at all? I foresee good times, a bright future. Does the Book have anything to say about the future, Gangadhar?

GANGADHAR: (*Reading from the Bible.*) The wolf also shall dwell with the lamb, and the leopard shall lie down with the kid; and the calf and the young lion and the fatling together; and a little child shall lead them. And the cow and the bear shall feed; their young ones shall lie down together; and the lion shall eat straw like the ox. And the suckling child shall play on the hole of the asp, and the weaned child shall put his hand on the cockatrice' den.

SUNDARDAS: Children, you've heard readings from both the Bhagavat and the Bible. Now listen to what I have to say. Sundardas foresees a golden era of peace and prosperity on earth. Injustice, disputes, lies and exploitation will disappear. Cows will come back home from the fields without having to be herded, countries will have no boundaries and homes no dividing walls. Everyone will be happy and live in plenty. All humanity will live as brothers and sisters. There will be no wars, no differences, no fights, no diseases, no suffering, no stealing, no lies, no adultery. Tigers and lambs will share the same watering hole. Lions and tigers will befriend human beings. Clouds will pour rain wherever there is need of water. Harvests will be golden. Human beings will realise that they're a part of God. Men and women will wear rich silk clothes and pray together without segregation and realise godhood. (*Pause.*) There's more that Sundardas is able to foresee. The Firinghees who now rule Orissa, after the Moghuls and the Marathas, will come to Sundardas.

Enter a young white SOLDIER, *as if on a cue. He seems to be in a hurry. He looks around.* SUNDARDAS *notices him, and a smile lights up his face. He continues.*

SUNDARDAS: The Firinghee will come and stand before Sundardas his head bowed.

Let alone bow his head, the SOLDIER *looks around with unconcealed insolence. He seems to be searching for somebody.*

SUNDARDAS: The Firinghee will come and bow his head before Sundardas.

No change in the SOLDIER*'s attitude.* SUNDARDAS *beckons to* RAMACHANDRA *and whispers something in his ear.* RAMACHANDRA *goes inside the hut. The* SOLDIER *continues his search and seems to zero in on* BALABHADRA. BALABHADRA *ducks behind a group of people, trying to escape. The* SOLDIER *looks for him. Meanwhile* RAMACHANDRA *brings* SUNDARDAS *an old battle fatigue which* SUNDARDAS *puts on. The* SOLDIER, *engrossed in his search, is completely unaware of what is happening. 'Attention!'* SUNDARDAS *commands in a booming voice. The* SOLDIER *is startled and salutes him.*

SUNDARDAS: The Firinghee will come and bow before Sundardas. (*The* SOLDIER *bows his head.*) The Firinghee will accept Sundardas as the only teacher and follow his precepts.

He pauses. There is silence.

SUNDERDAS: Children, did you see that? The young white boy here became afraid because of how I am dressed. Now, what does that teach you? This: that we see only the clothes, the exterior, and not what is within. Unless we go beyond clothes, unless we cast them aside, how can we journey within? How can we realise ourselves? (*He takes off the uniform.*) Learn to ignore how people are dressed. Whether I wear these clothes or others, I remain who I am: Sundardas. Think of clay. You can make all sorts of things out of it—bowls, pitchers, plates and cups. Only the names are different, the basic material remains the same. The clay is fundamental to them all, the clay is the truth; the pitchers and vessels are only forms. You must be able to see the clay in them. Just as you must recognise yourselves underneath what you wear. (*Pauses. Raising his hand, he plucks a flower out of air.*) Look at this flower. Just as it has several petals, the human mind too has several layers, several forms; each encloses the mind like a petal. (*He plucks a petal.*) The commands of parents. (*Plucks another petal.*) The advice of elders. (*Plucks yet another.*) The guru's teachings. (*Another petal goes.*) The priest's injunctions. (*Another petal.*) The social code. (*Looks at the flower in his hand.*) Only one more petal is left. What is it—the soul? Or just another form, a covering, an influence? Let's throw that one away too. (*Lets it drop.*) So what remains? What remains is the *atman.* Nothing, you might say, there's nothing. But that nothingness is the *atman.* The Brahman is nothingness. How can one describe nothingness? One cannot ever describe what it is, one can only say what it is not. The Brahman is not you or I. It has no shape, no length, no breadth, no boundaries. It's not creation, nor conservation, nor destruction. Neither male, nor female. Not will, not time. Not striving, nor desire. Not memory, nor roots; not theories, nor explanations, whether subtle or crude; not scriptures, not holy books. Not castes or creeds; not colours or shapes. Not light, nor darkness. Not one, not many. Not the beginning, nor the end. Not birth, not living, not death. Not writing, not the writer. Not the doer, nor the deed. Not heaven, nor hell. Neither good nor bad. Neither right nor wrong. Not emotion, not devotion. Not salvation, not liberation. Not the achiever, not the achievement. Not samadhi, not yoga. Not disease. Not sleep nor wakefulness, not dreams either. There's nothing in the Brahman. It is not anywhere, not in anything. Once in northern India there was a holy man named Kabir who said:

Not in centres of pilgrimage,
Not in idols, not in solitary abodes,
Not in mosques, nor in temples,
Not in Kashi, nor in Kailash.

Kabir mentioned mosques because we know about mosques; the Muslims had been around for a long time. But now a new people have come to us—the Firinghees. How many years ago did they arrive, Gangadhar?

GANGADHAR: Twenty-three.

SUNDARDAS: Twenty-three years already? How quickly time passes. The Firinghees have a religion of their own just as the Muslims do. Gangadhar, enlighten these children about how we came to know about the Firinghee religion.

GANGADHAR: The Christian padres started preaching their religion in this country a couple of years ago. They printed books and distributed them to people in the crowded marketplaces. Once Krupasindhu got a book of questions and answers from these people when he went to the Tangi market. This was a Catechism. When Radhu Das went to Cuttack to buy sugar, he found a padre distributing a book called the Ten Commandments in Chowdhury Bazaar and brought a copy back.

SUNDARDAS: When I read those books I nearly danced with joy. Children, I said, what a treasure you've got me at last! This is it! These are the basic things. The ethics, the rules of the right way to live. Then my boys went looking for the padres and collected from them the Old Testament, the New Testament, the Gospels. But there's nothing to beat this one book—the Ten Commandments. All the rules of good behaviour have been reduced to just ten. Sundardas too had spoken of these things before, but not with the same lucidity and clarity. Gangadhar, recite the ten Commandments.

GANGADHAR: The Ten Commandments of the Lord are: I am the Lord thy God, thou shalt have no other gods before me. Thou shalt not make unto thee any graven image, thou shalt not bow down thyself to them. Thou shalt not take the name of the Lord thy God in vain. Remember the sabbath day, to keep it holy. Honour thy father and thy mother. Thou shalt not kill. Thou shalt not commit adultery. Thou shalt not steal. Thou shalt not bear false witness against thy neighbour. Thou shalt not covet thy neighbour's house, wife, manservant, maidservant nor his goods.

SUNDARDAS: How wonderful, how true! It feels good just to hear them over and over again. So I began telling people about these commandments. And I told my disciples: Sons, go spread the good word. Gangadhar, tell me: Krupasindhu and Radhu Das were supposed to leave yesterday to preach the Ten Commandments, did they go?

GANGADHAR: Yes, they did, Baba.

SUNDARDAS: (*Turns to DEVIKA.*) Has Krupasindhu left?

DEVIKA: Yes, Baba.

SUNDARDAS: Oh, we've completely forgotten our Firinghee soldier. (*Turns to him.*) Young man, what brings you here?

MARUA: He might be looking for his horse.

The SOLDIER *looks on uncomprehendingly.*

MARUA: Spill it out, Moonface. Tell us what or who you're looking for.

SOLDIER: (*Speaks in a clipped soldierly style.*) I'm looking for a native infantry soldier who has run away after beating the commissioner's horse-cab driver with a stick.

SUNDARDAS: There doesn't seem to be any native soldier around here.

The SOLDIER *stares into the faces and grabs BALABHADRA, mistaking him for the runaway soldier.* BUDA MUNDA *and* RATANA PANA *grab* BALABHADRA*'s free arm and pull him towards them. After a few pulls and counter-pulls, the soldier glares at the tribesmen in anger, draws his pistol and chases them away. The two men run for dear life and never return. The* SOLDIER *stares into* BALABHADRA*'s face closely and decides he's not the man he's looking* *for, shakes his head and lets* BALABHADRA *go. Saluting* SUNDARDAS, *he exits.*

MARUA: Goodbye, Moonface. Go in peace. Hope you soon run into your horse and the missing native soldier.

SUNDARDAS: That takes care of the hill thugs and the soldier. Does anyone else here have a problem?

KAMALI: Baba, my husband beats me regularly. He says our child perished because we stopped worshipping idols. But I say God took back our child. Let my husband follow his faith and leave me to mine. Am I not right, Baba?

SUNDARDAS: Absolutely.

KAMALI: My husband has threatened to kill me if I don't go back to worshipping idols. And my father beats my mother for the same reason.

DAANI: They treat us like cats and dogs, Baba. They tie us up and beat the life out of us.

SUNDARDAS: Praise be to you, mother. One must suffer to remain true to one's faith. Think what Jesus Christ went through. You'll find God, I tell you. There are good days ahead.

DAANI: May your words come true, Baba.

SUNDARDAS: Of course they will. (*Looks at* BRAHMIN I.) Shall we then begin our discussion of the scriptures?

BRAHMIN I *raises a finger and goes away to relieve himself.*

SUNDARDAS: (*Looks at* BRAHMIN II.) Stay here until your friend comes back. Only a little while ago you were in splits about horses. Do you know what the Brihadaranyak Upanishad has to say?

BRAHMIN II *shakes his head.*

SUNDARDAS: The human body is a chariot and the senses are horses.

BRAHMIN II *tucks his sacred thread around his ear indicating that he also needs to relieve himself.*

SUNDARDAS: The atman rides the chariot; wisdom is the charioteer and the mind is the land over which the chariot rolls.

BRAHMIN II *makes his escape at the first opportunity.* SUNDARDAS *looks up at the sun; it is late in the day. He looks around and finds* MARUA *collecting the petals from the ground.* SUNDARDAS *gives her a smile and plucks another flower from the air and is about to present it to her.*

Enter KRUPASINDHU SAHU *and* RADHU DAS, *screaming and crying: 'We were almost killed.' They prostrate themselves before* SUNDARDAS. *He picks them up lovingly and pats them on the back.* DEVIKA, KRUPASINDHU*'s wife, attends to her husband.* SUNDARDAS *attends to* RADHU DAS.

SUNDARDAS: Woe is me, what am I witnessing? Krupasindhu, who has reduced you to such a state, my son? Who subjected my poor Radhu to such torture?

RADHU DAS: Baba, we went to Bhairavpur yesterday to preach the Ten Commandments. It seems only a few days ago a mad padre had been there to preach Christianity and the villagers had chased him out of the village. The moment we started preaching they began to call us names. I warned Krupasindhu that we'd do well to leave, but he wouldn't budge until he had recited the commandments.

KRUPASINDHU: By then the villagers had armed themselves with sticks and rocks. We've chased out a white padre, they shouted, we know how to deal with Blackies; you're no match for us. Then they fell upon us and started beating us within an inch of our lives. But the more they beat the louder I went on about the commandments.

SUNDARDAS: That's terrible, a grave injustice. Gangadhar and

Ramachandra, go to Cuttack and inform the padres. We must consult with them. Tell them that Sundardas wants them to come to Kujibar at once. Let them see with their own eyes the plight my children have suffered as a result of preaching their Ten Commandments. Let them tell us how we should go about it. Children, carry Krupasindhu and Radhu Das inside. Take care of them.

The disciples carry KRUPASINDHU *and* RADHU DAS *inside.* SUNDARDAS *notices the flower in his hand and gives it to* MARUA. *Everyone watches him with deep respect and fascination.*

Scene II

Kujibar ashram. Early morning. The place has been swept clean and adorned with flowers. A cloth has been spread out on the platform. SUNDARDAS *himself is supervising the arrangements. The place is crowded.*

SUNDARDAS: Children, bring another sheet and spread it out. The padres said they'd arrive early in the morning, didn't they?

RAMACHANDRA: That's what they said, Baba. They must have set out already; they should be arriving any time now. Gangadhar stayed back to escort them.

SUNDARDAS: Good. Good. What else did the padres say?

RAMACHANDRA: In the evening when they said their prayers we too knelt on the floor, bowed our heads and joined them in worship.

SUNDARDAS: Worship? What was that like?

RAMACHANDRA: One of them began to read aloud from the Book and the rest listened in silence.

SUNDARDAS: That's fine. Did you see the padre who came here?

RAMACHANDRA: No, not him. We saw Padre Lacey and Padre Sutton in Cuttack. There we learned that the padre who came here was Bampton. He lives in Puri, but is forever on the move from place to place on horseback. Cuttack today, Ganjam tomorrow. People have started calling him the Horseman Padre.

SUNDARDAS: An appropriate name too.

Voices outside. Enter GANGADHAR *with* LACEY *and* SUTTON, *both dressed in full padre gear.* SUNDARDAS *prostrates himself before them. The padres pick him up and shake his hand.* SUNDARDAS *welcomes them and leads them to the platform.*

SUNDARDAS: Welcome! Welcome! Welcome to Kujibar ashram! We are fortunate to have the dust from your feet in our humble abode!

LACEY: Let me introduce us. My name is Charles Lacey. I live in Cuttack. (*Points to* SUTTON.) He is Amos Sutton. He lives in Balasore, but visits Cuttack every so often.

SUNDARDAS: Very well, very well. So the Company has posted you to Cuttack and him to Balasore?

SUTTON: (*With emphasis.*) No, no, we're not employees of the Company. We have nothing to do with it.

LACEY: The East India Company's men are the white collectors, magistrates, police and soldiers you see around. We've been sent by the General Baptist Mission of England. The Company is our foe, not our friend. Some time ago the Company wouldn't even allow missionaries to live within its territory. That's why the people of the Mission took up residence in Serampore, near Calcutta, on Danish territory. We got permission to preach on the Company's territory only fifteen years ago. The first preacher who arrived in Orissa from Serampore was Brother William Bampton. He went to live in Puri. I came here three years ago, then came Brother Sutton.

SUNDARDAS: A welcome event.

LACEY: When we came to Orissa idol worship was not the only barbaric practice we witnessed. We had heard of widows immolating themselves on the burning pyres of their husbands, and Brother Bampton actually saw one instance of this with his own eyes, when a young Brahmin widow committed sati. I myself saw another, a seventeen-year-old Bengali widow. As she burnt to death people shouted: 'Glory to Lord Jagannath'!

SUNDARDAS: What barbarity!

SUTTON: Yet another barbaric practice was people committing suicide by throwing themselves under the wheels of Jagannath's chariot. Brother Bampton once happened upon a body. Dogs were tearing it to pieces, but nobody seemed to bother.

SUNDARDAS: How horrible!

LACEY: During the last chariot festival, just three months ago, Brother Sutton and I saw a man throw himself under the chariot wheels. He was cut into two. Instead of condemning it, people praised the dead man's devotion and piety!

SUNDARDAS: That's horrendous! A matter of deep sorrow. The temple priests play a large role in all this, let me tell you.

SUTTON: I've nicknamed them the carrion-eaters of Puri. Their only passion is to bleed the pilgrims dry. They never bother about their welfare. Thousands of pilgrims succumb to disease during the chariot festival every year and Puri simply bursts at the seams with dead bodies, but no one bothers about it!

SUNDARDAS: You do. May God crown your efforts with success.

SUTTON: When I arrived in India I found the heat unbearable. 110 degrees! I had never seen so many black people. They all went around half-naked; they sat in the dust and ate with their fingers. I thought to myself, oh God, do I have to live out the rest of my life in the midst of these creatures! But after a while I got used to it—the people, the climate, the place.

SUNDARDAS: Your Oriya is so good! How is everything with your family?

SUTTON: As soon as I reached Cuttack last year, Charlotte fell ill. We took her to Puri hoping that the change of air would do her good, but she left me for God. (*He wipes his eyes.*) We had been married only a year.

SUNDARDAS: How sad!

SUTTON: All God's will.

LACEY: We are curious about you, we would like to know something about you.

SUNDARDAS: My name is Sundardas. I don't know my age. Some say I am one hundred years old, but that could easily be an exaggeration. I was once a soldier, the commander of the army in the kingdom of Athgarh. Those days I was fond of big game hunting and would go into the forest whenever I had the chance. One time, when I shot an arrow into a doe, a voice arose within me: Abandon this path, follow the path of truth and piety, that is the right path for you.

LACEY: Something similar had happened to St Paul on the road to Damascus. He received a divine message.

SUNDARDAS: I left Athgarh the same day and came here. At that time there was nothing here. Only a stunted banyan tree, under which I meditated. It took me years but I found the truth I was looking for.

SUTTON: Was that the truth of Hinduism?

SUNDARDAS: Hinduism is unlike your religion. You have only one holy book, but we have several—the Vedas, the Vedants, the Upanishads, the Gita. There are people in the hills who don't have written scriptures. The Hindu religion takes on several forms.

LACEY: But all of you believe in idol worship.

SUNDARDAS: I am opposed to it, although I'm a Hindu. You'll not find a single idol in my ashram. For me, a Hindu is someone who follows the path of righteousness.

SUTTON: Hinduism is based on the caste system.

SUNDARDAS: Not here, not in this ashram. No one here belongs to any caste; no one is an untouchable here. Of course, originally they are all from different castes: Ramachandra Jachak is a kshatriya, his father Hariwat Rao was a Maratha soldier. Krupasindhu Sahu is a weaver, Sudarshan Raut a peasant, Radhu Das a karan, Daitari Nayak an astrologer. There are three Gangadhars here—Gangadhar Sarangi, Gangadhar Mohanty and Gangadhar Biswal. The first is a brahmin, the second a karan and the third a peasant. And Marua here, she says she has no caste: she belongs to the female caste. We have no restrictions on intermingling; we live together, we eat together.

SUTTON: How do Hindus react to all this?

SUNDARDAS: They don't approve. But I tell them: look at clothes drying in the sun, all different colours and sorts, belonging to different people; some people might feel they will become polluted if they touch each other, but does the sun think that? Does the sun make any distinction, does the sun discriminate? It dries them all equally well. Everyone is equal in God's eyes. Who are we to create castes, distinctions, divisions?

LACEY: What kind of teaching you give your disciples?

SUNDARDAS: I tell them: Children, learn, keep an open mind, fill your heart with true knowledge and wisdom. Read the Hindu scriptures, but read the Christians' New Testament as well. Where else will you find someone like Jesus Christ? One person is condemned to swing at the end of the rope but another person comes forward to take his place. That's Jesus Christ for you. Children, that's the greatest act of all. You've got everything here on earth – food, clothes, wisdom. Food will rot, clothes will tear, but wisdom will stay forever. No one can destroy it. Seek it, make it yours. Money won't buy it, but suffering will. Yearn for it, my children.

SUTTON: Your disciples preach the Ten Commandments. What do you think of the Commandments?

SUNDARDAS: I preached much the same thing even before I read your book. Don't covet, don't commit adultery, don't worship idols, et cetera. But there I found all the rules nicely grouped together. I immediately realised that spreading the Ten Commandments would be the mission of my life. And so I started sending people out into the countryside.

SUTTON: The Ten Commandments hold the key to our religion too. We heard that your disciples were beaten up when they tried to preach them.

SUNDARDAS: Yes, that's why I asked you to come. What should we do if our people are attacked when they spread God's word?

LACEY: You're not alone in receiving such rough treatment. We too have had our share: people throw rocks, stones and cow dung at us, they drive cattle into our meetings to disrupt them. Of course ignoramuses put our Lord Jesus Christ to no mean suffering. But

Jesus said: Blessed are they which are persecuted for righteousness' sake: for theirs is the kingdom of heaven. Blessed are ye, when men shall revile you, and persecute you, and shall say all manner of evil against you falsely, for my sake.

SUNDARDAS: How wonderful! Did you hear that, Gangadhar and Ramachandra? Call Krupasindhu and Radhu Das so that they too might hear it. They are blessed since they have received beatings while preaching Christ's teachings. They shall inherit heaven. Glory to Jesus Christ. Gangadhar, do you have anything to ask the padres?

GANGADHAR: Baba, what shall we do about Balabhadra?

SUNDARDAS: (*To* LACEY.) You were talking about the practices of Hindus. But there are also the hill people. They practice human sacrifice.

LACEY: We've heard about that and intend to reach them soon the Lord's word.

SUNDARDAS: (*Points to* BALABHADRA.) This boy narrowly escaped being sacrificed. He's staying with us now.

GANGADHAR: He does not wish to remain here any longer.

LACEY: Send him with us, we'll take care of him. We'll put him to our school. And we request you to start a school here. If you're willing to run it, we'll be happy to build it.

SUNDARDAS: That's an excellent idea. But let Gangadhar visit your school first. I have a suggestion too. Build a place to stay beside my ashram; you could spend at least a month or two here, if not the whole time. It would be much to our benefit.

SUTTON: Thank you for the suggestion. We will think about it. But we need to settle down in Cuttack. We have already bought a piece of land there to build a chapel. With your help we could build a place to stay here, and a church too.

SUNDARDAS: That would be fine.

SUTTON: I'm trying to write an Oriya grammar and I might need your help.

SUNDARDAS: Certainly. Children, any other questions to the padres?

MARUA *comes forward.*

MARUA: You preach the Ten Commandments out in the countryside. Why don't you first try to convince the Firinghee collectors, magistrates and commanders?

SUNDARDAS: Previously Marua worked in a Firinghee sahib's home, but left when she could stand it no longer. She has been excommunicated by her kinsmen, expelled from her caste.

LACEY: Send her with us. She can help us take care of the girls in the school.

SUNDARDAS: You are taking a son and a daughter from me.

LACEY: You have plenty others.

SUNDARDAS: Still. Every child is dear to his parents. Well, Gangadhar, what about something to eat? Is everything arranged? The padres will eat with us.

LACEY: Oh no, we don't want to inconvenience you. It's time we left.

SUTTON: (*Presents* SUNDARDAS *a shawl.*) Please accept this little present.

SUNDARDAS: You are our guests, and leaving without a bite. On top of it, you're giving me a present. But I can you give you nothing. (*Thoughtful pause.*) Gangadhar is the best among my disciples, my favourite. And the most learned too. I like him more than all the others. He's like my right hand. (*Places his hand on* GANGADHAR*'s shoulder.*) I'm an ascetic and possess nothing that I can offer you as a present. I'm giving Gangadhar to you. He will help you preach.

GANGADHAR: (*Surprised.*) Baba!

SUNDARDAS: Go with them, son. I will come to Cuttack and see you sometimes.

SUNDARDAS *raises his hand and blesses them.* LACEY *and* SUTTON *prostrate themselves before* SUNDARDAS *and he picks them up and pumps their hands.* LACEY *and* SUTTON *leave with* BALABHADRA, MARUA and GANGADHAR. *The rest watch them until they're out of sight.*

ACT TWO

Scene I

The VILLAGERS *on the road. 'The Firinghees are coming!' someone shouts, and they all scatter. 'It's only some padres!' announces someone else, and they regroup. Enter* LACEY *and* GANGADHAR.

LACEY: Greetings, brothers and sisters!
GANGADHAR: (*Whispers to* LACEY.) There aren't any women here.
LACEY: Sorry. Greetings, brothers! We've come to preach the Gospel of Jesus Christ.
VILLAGER: Go ahead and begin.
LACEY: Our friend Gangadhar here will start with the Ten Commandments.
VILLAGER: No, no. We want you to start.
VILLAGER I: Yes, let's have it from the Firinghee's mouth first.
LACEY: As you wish, brothers. Let me begin with a psalm. (*Sings.*) Unto thee lift I up mine eyes, O thou that dwellest in the heavens.
VILLAGER: Hail Hari! Glory to the Lord!
LACEY: Jesus Christ said: I dwell in him who eats my flesh and drinks my blood.
VILLAGER: What! Eat Christ's flesh and drink his blood! Are you people monsters?

Noise.

LACEY: (*Raises his voice.*) The meaning is that to keep your faith alive you need to keep feeding it, and there's only one nourishment for twice-born souls: Jesus Christ. All God's children must hunger for him. Without him they will grow weak and sad, and attain nothing. So approach Jesus Christ with trust and accept him as the only food for the soul. Are you able to follow me?

VILLAGER: Only too well, but go on. Explain some more.

LACEY: The soul is different from the body. The body nourishes itself through the mouth, but the soul derives sustenance from Christ through prayer, humility, meditation, faith, love and gratitude. If someone comes and tells me, look, there will be a big feast but you will only be allowed to look at the spread, will that satisfy me? Unless one actually partakes of the food, what good is it to the body? It's the same with the soul. It needs the body and blood of Jesus Christ for faith and devotion to grow. Do you understand?

VILLAGER: Every word.

LACEY: So put your faith in Jesus Christ. He will forgive you.

VILLAGER: (*Mockingly.*) All right, we believe in your Jesus Christ. There. Now, has he forgiven us?

GANGADHAR: This is not something to make fun of.

VILLAGER: No, no, this is manna from heaven, and we are eating it up.

LACEY: Jesus said to pray as follows: Our Father which art in heaven, Hallowed be thy name. Thy kingdom come. Thy will be done in earth, as it is in heaven. Give us this day our daily bread. And forgive us our debts, as we forgive our debtors. And lead us not into temptation, but deliver us from evil: For thine is the kingdom, and the power, and the glory, for ever. Amen.

VILLAGER: Look, if you're free to commit your sins and pray to your Jesus Christ, then we can commit our own and pray to our gods.

LACEY: But which god will you pray to?

VILLAGER: To whoever takes our fancy. We don't exactly want for gods, you know.

LACEY: But you know what happens to someone with his feet in two boats?

VILLAGER: Of course. The fool will drown.

LACEY: So will you if you pray to several gods. Put your faith in one god. He who believes in one god will receive eternal bliss.

VILLAGER: Our Brahman is one.

LACEY: Where is your Brahman?

VILLAGER: Within us.

LACEY: God doesn't reside within the human body. (*He takes out his pocket watch and holds it close to a villager's ear.*) This watch is ticking, its hands moving. Does that mean the creator of the watch is inside it?

VILLAGER: Give it to us and we'll tell you.

The VILLAGERS *take it out of* LACEY*'s hand and pass it around.* LACEY *and* GANGADHAR *retrieve it with considerable effort.*

LACEY: Now Gangadhar will recite the Ten Commandments.

VILLAGER: All right. It's the black padre's turn. The white one is already tired out.

VILLAGER: So what are these Ten Commandments?

GANGADHAR: God Almighty gave them to Moses.

VILLAGER: What! Your god gave them to a mouse?

GANGADHAR: No, to Moses. He could see the future. Thou shalt have no other gods before me. Thou shalt not make unto thee any graven image, or any likeness of any thing that is in heaven above, or that is in the earth beneath, or that is in the water under the earth: Thou shalt not bow down thyself to them, nor serve them: for I the Lord thy God am a jealous God, visiting the iniquity of the fathers upon the children unto the third and fourth generation of them that hate me . . .

VILLAGER: If that's what your god said to your mouse, then that's good enough for you, but we're happy with our gods. We'll continue to worship them. Why shouldn't we?

LACEY: Your gods are all false. They're made of stone and wood.

VILLAGER: For us they're living gods.

LACEY: Your idols are silver and gold, the work of men's hands. They have mouths, but they speak not: eyes have they, but they see not. They have ears, but they hear not: noses they have, but they smell not. They have hands, but they handle not: feet have they, but they walk not: neither speak they through their throat. They that make them are like unto them; so is every one that trusteth in them.

VILLAGER: If our gods are nothing, who is running the universe?

LACEY: God the Father.

VILLAGER: That's just it. Because God the Father can't be everywhere at the same time, He has sent out other gods, like Jagannath, Krishna, Ram and Balaram. The same way as your Company of England does. The Company remains in England, but sends judges, magistrates and police here.

LACEY: The Company sends its men to collect revenue, to administer justice. But still the Company is a human creation. And a human being can only be in one place at any given time. But God is omnipresent, omniscient. He is everywhere. He knows everything. Those of us who live in Cuttack do not have an inkling of what's happening in Puri, do we? But God has. God does not need underlings. You said Jagannath, Krishna, Ram and Balaram are all God's deputies. Now take the Company's men—the judges, the magistrates, the police. Can they hope to keep their jobs if they act according to their own wishes rather than follow the Company's rules and regulations? Can your lesser gods lose their jobs the same way?

VILLAGER: What nonsense you're talking. Ram, Balaram, Jagannath aren't the employees of god. God is like a king. Just as a king has to go around at night in disguise to find out the true state of affairs, god takes the forms of Ram and Krishna.

LACEY: God is only one, not many.

A PUNDIT *elbows his way through the crowd and confronts* LACEY.

PUNDIT: Your scriptures might say that there's only one god, but ours say there are many paths to Him.

LACEY: Your scriptures are false.

PUNDIT: Why do you think they're false? After all, our god gave them to us.

LACEY: Can there be impure water in a clean, pure river? God is pure. Would he give us anything impure?

PUNDIT: No.

LACEY: Your scriptures are unholy, they're false—they aren't a gift from God. Your scriptures cannot save you. Our scripture came straight from God. It alone can cleanse the mind, wipe away sins. Think about that.

PUNDIT: Maybe. But our scriptures make as much sense to us as yours to you. Our ancestors found salvation by reading them; who am I to question them? Stop speaking against our scriptures.

LACEY: Our ancestors too worshipped idols; they too practised human sacrifice. But their children received the light and gave up those abominable practices. All I ask is that you subject your scriptures to close scrutiny so that you will know the truth.

PUNDIT: Firinghee, you tread in your path, I will tread in mine. Goodbye.

Exit PUNDIT.

VILLAGER: That's right, you worship your Christ and we'll worship our Krishna. He'll save us.

GANGADHAR: Ha, the same Krishna who couldn't save himself from the arrows of Jara the hill man?

LACEY: Your Krishna was a sinner. He sinned with sixteen hundred Gopi girls.

VILLAGERS: What, badmouthing Lord Krishna? Seize the wretches!

GANGADHAR: Calm down, calm down. Just listen to us.

VILLAGERS: This black Brahmin has been eating the crumbs and leftovers of the padres. Hit him!

VILLAGER: Beat them! Lynch them!

The VILLAGERS *push and shove* LACEY *and* GANGADHAR, *forcing them to abandon preaching.*

Scene II

The village road. A crowd of villagers. Enter BAMPTON, *singing loudly.*

BAMPTON:

If not our sweet lord Jesus Christ
Who else can save?
The world is a cesspool of sin
And our lord is the only redeemer.
Jesus Christ, the son of God!
Pray to him and save your soul!

Brothers, put your faith in Jesus Christ. (*He notices a lone woman in the crowd.*) Sorry. Sister and brothers, put your faith in Jesus Christ. He will save you all.

VILLAGER: Before he saves us, let's see what he looks like. Show us your Jesus Christ.

BAMPTON: The Lord is in His heaven.

VILLAGER: So go and ask him to show himself. We must see him before we can put our faith in him.

BAMPTON: It's not necessary to see Him. When a doctor comes to give medicine to a man in the grip of a fever, who's shaking and shivering in agony, does he first demand to see the fever? What will happen to the man if the doctor is so foolish? He'll die, won't he?

VILLAGER: Of course he will.

BAMPTON: It's the same with Jesus Christ. If you wait until you've seen Him to put your trust in Him, you'll die first. (*Pause.*) Jesus alone can save your soul. Put your faith in Him.

VILLAGER: Oh no. We have our own gods to save our souls—Krishna, Ram, Brahma, Vishnu, Maheswar.

BAMPTON: Brothers and sister, you couldn't be more mistaken. God created everything for a purpose. He created the sun, for example, to provide light and warmth. Is it possible for anyone to spurn the sun God created and create one of his own? Does anyone reject rice and live on sand and stone? The same way God sent Jesus Christ as our saviour. As with the sun, so with the Lord. (*Sings* 'Who else can save'.)

VILLAGER: We know all that. Invoking Ram's name will wipe away our sins. *Ra* empties the mind of all sinful thoughts, *ma* prevents all future sins. The same with Govinda's name. The name alone is enough to save us.

BAMPTON: Only repeating God's name won't help, that won't save you from punishment. Suppose you borrow one hundred rupees from a moneylender, spend it and are no longer in a position to repay the money. When the moneylender hounds you, do you tell him: Sir, true I have no money to repay you, but I am ready to repeat your name forever and sing your praises? Will he let you off? Suppose you don't pay the land revenue taxes. Will you tell the collector that you'll chant his name? Do you steal and when you're caught tell the magistrate that you're ready to repeat his name? Do you hope that the collector or the magistrate will set you free? No, he'll send you to jail. That's why I tell you that just invoking God's name isn't enough. You have to believe in Jesus Christ.

VILLAGER: We believe in our gods because we're able to see them in our temples. How can we believe in Jesus Christ if we haven't seen him?

VILLAGER: These Firinghees don't have temples. What sort of religion is that?

BAMPTON: Tell me—do you obey the governor general? Do you respect him?

VILLAGER: Of course we do.

BAMPTON: Have any of you seen him?

VILLAGER: No, but we've heard a lot about him.

BAMPTON: Have a little patience, and I'll tell you all about Jesus Christ.

VILLAGER: First of all, tell us whether he's dark-skinned or fair.

BAMPTON: (*Angry, irritated.*) What does that matter?

VILLAGER: Now, now, don't fly off the handle. Our Krishna was dark. What colour was your Christ?

VILLAGER: Look at the poor bugger! He doesn't even know whether Jesus Christ was fair or dark, but see how eager he is to talk about him!

VILLAGER: Never mind. (*Turns to* BAMPTON.) Speak.

BAMPTON: Humble yourselves therefore under the mighty hand of God, that he may exalt you in due time: Casting all your care upon him; for he careth for you. Be sober, be vigilant; because your adversary the devil, as a roaring lion, walketh about, seeking whom he may devour: Whom resist steadfast in the faith, knowing that the same afflictions are accomplished in your brethren that are in the world. But the God of all grace, who hath called us unto his eternal glory by Christ Jesus, after that ye have suffered a while, make you perfect, establish, strengthen, settle you. To him be glory and dominion for ever and ever. Amen. Now let me explain.

VILLAGER: No need to, we understood every word.

VILLAGER: We had no problem understanding, you speak Oriya very well.

VILLAGER: Try Sanskrit some time.

VILLAGER: Or your own language—the Firinghee tongue.

BAMPTON: All right, I'll try a little something in English. For God so loved the world that he gave his only begotten Son, that whoever believeth in Him should not perish, but have everlasting life.

VILLAGER: (*Turns to* a villager FAKIRA.) Hey, you there, Fakira. Did you understand that? You've learnt English, haven't you?

VILLAGER: Explain it in Oriya, padre, will you?

BAMPTON: Loved god the world so much he his only begotten son gave away, not perisheth he who in him believeth but receiveth life everlasting. Clear?

VILLAGER: Crystal clear! Hey Fakira, try your English on the padre, why don't you?

FAKIRA: (*Shyly.*) Never mind.

VILLAGER: You woman of a man! You only know how to show off to us! In front of the padre you become as quiet as a mouse. Come on, show the Firinghee that we aren't dimwits.

FAKIRA: You want me to? All right, here I go! (*He rattles off in a singsong voice.*) Dear Sir, I have the honour to acquaint you that I am sick by the fever this for cannot stand nor walk neither rise from slip but pass yesterday at evening here did you order if you will go tomorrow then I will give you some physic and I cannot go for my misfortune and did not cure therefore I pray before you I am very poor man and orphan so gracious grant me grace to avoid from this fever and always to be nourished as any room I am sir your most obedient humble servant Fukeer Chunder Dass.

VILLAGER: Splendid! But did the padre understand you?

VILLAGER: It's getting late. (*Turn to* BAMPTON.) Come on, distribute your books and be done with it. It's time to go home.

BAMPTON: I don't have any books. Brother Sutton will give you some next time.

VILLAGER: What, if you didn't have books to distribute, why the hell have you wasted our time?

VILLAGER: (*Tugs at* BAMPTON*'s bag.*) Look in the padre's bag.

VILLAGER: Give us your horse then. Surely a padre can't be attached to material things!

BAMPTON: It's not attachment to keep what one needs. Sorry, I can't give away my horse.

VILLAGER: You don't have any books, you won't give us the horse. What are you good for, eh—only lectures? You're asking for a roughing-up.

The VILLAGERS *surround* BAMPTON, *who tries to run away. They playfully chase him a good distance.*

VILLAGERS: Hit him with rocks! Pelt the padre with cow dung, shards and stones.

VILLAGERS: Hail Hari! Glory to Hari!

The commotion continues for a while.

Scene III

The VILLAGERS *out on the road, mimicking the padres.*

VILLAGER I: Brothers and sisters, here are the books. Take them, they're yours for free. The Gospel according to Luke, the Gospel according to Mathew, the Gospel according to Mark, the Gospel according to John, the Bible, the Ten Commendments, the Book of Catechism.

VILLAGER *distributes dry leaves.*

VILLAGER I: Listen to God's own words; listen to the Ten Commandments. Thou shalt not take the name of the Lord thy God in vain; for the Lord will not hold him guiltless that taketh his name in vain.

VILLAGERS: Hail Hari! Hail Hari!

VILLAGER: Folks, I think I can see a padre headed this way.

VILLAGER I: Let him come, but you're going to hear the Ten Commandments only from me.

Enter SUTTON. VILLAGER I *continues his spiel, ignoring him completely.*

VILLAGER I: Thou shalt kill, thou shalt commit all abominations, thou shalt steal and stand false witness against thy neighbour, thou shalt covet thy neighbour's wife and maids and cattle and donkeys and whatever else he has!

SUTTON*'s face clouds over; he looks askance at the speaker. The speaker simply adds: 'Never do any of the above' and the crowd breaks into peals of laughter. After the laughter subsides,* SUTTON *clears his throat.*

SUTTON: Take these books, brothers and sisters, they're all for free. The Gospel according to St Luke, the Gospel according to

St Mathew, the Gospel according to St Mark, the Gospel according to St John, the Bible, the Ten Commandments, the Book of Catechism.

VILLAGER I: (*To one of his companions.*) This padre is definitely on the Company's payroll. What else could explain distributing books for free? After all, our village astrologer demands a hefty fee just for scratching a few lines on a palm-leaf!

VILLAGER: Let's ask the padre.

VILLAGER I: (*Turns to* SUTTON.) These books you're giving away—haven't they been printed by the Company? How much does the Company pay you to distribute them?

SUTTON: These are not the Company's books; they've been printed by the Baptist Mission. The good and the devout people of our country have paid the cost of printing. And they're being distributed free for your benefit.

VILLAGER: But why should the good people of your country waste their good money on the good people of our country?

SUTTON: Good Christians that they are they want the words of Christ to reach all corners of the earth.

VILLAGER: Say, what's your salary?

SUTTON: (*Irritated.*) What does that matter?

VILLAGER: Frankly, it doesn't. Just a bit of information.

SUTTON: We get what little we need for our food and clothing.

VILLAGER: (*To his companions.*) Poor wretch! Doesn't he get enough food in his own country not to have to come here?

SUTTON *distributes the books without further arguments.*

VILLAGER: Why don't you distribute some hashish instead of these silly books?

SUTTON: What! What did you say?

VILLAGER: Your head!

SUTTON: (*Holding his head with both hands.*) My head?

VILLAGER: What have you got inside your head?

SUTTON: Knowledge, the knowledge of the Holy Book—the New Testament.

VILLAGER: Read something from it. Let's hear you read.

SUTTON: (*Reads.*) Professing themselves to be wise, they became fools. And changed the glory of the uncorruptible God into an image made like to corruptible man, and to birds, and fourfooted beasts, and creeping things. Wherefore God also gave them up to uncleanness through the lusts of their own hearts, to dishonour their bodies between themselves: Who changed the truth of God into a lie, and worshipped and served the creature more than the Creator, who is blessed for ever. Amen.

VILLAGER: Now go ahead and explain it.

SUTTON: Idol worship, which you practice, is a sin. God does not reside in wood, in stones, or in temples.

VILLAGER: You mean there aren't any images of your gods?

SUTTON: Of course not.

VILLAGER: Who do you worship in your temples?

SUTTON: We have no temples.

VILLAGER: And no Brahmins either?

SUTTON: That's right—no Brahmins.

VILLAGER: What, no priests, no temples? What kind of a religion is that? You seem quite irreligious!

SUTTON: Ours is the only true faith, all others are false. Your gods Ram, Krishna, Vishnu and Mahadev are all false gods.

VILLAGER: What sinful words! Hail Hari! Hail Jagannath!

SUTTON: Your Lord Jagannath is just a grotesque idol carved out of a block of wood. Eighteen years ago when Jagannath needed a change of body, it was the Company that doled out the five thousand rupees. Let another eighteen years pass and you'll have to make another idol. And who do you think will fork out the money once again? The Company! It's the Company's money that will pay for the wood your Jagannath is carved out of; the Company will pay the carpenters and the painters. So what it all boils down to is this: your Lord Jagannath is a piece of painted wood owned by the Company!

VILLAGER: If Lord Jagannath is just a lump of wood, why do people from all over the world come to Him? If He is nothing, why do people worship Him? Why is the Company wasting its precious money on renewing His images? Why is it paying for the cloth which covers His chariot? Why is it collecting the pilgrim tax at the Eighteen Sluice Bridge?

SUTTON: We are not the Company's men, and according to us the Company is totally wrong to do all this.

VILLAGER: So go set your Company straight. You're asking us to give Him up when even your Company can't. Lord Jagannath is our living god; He is our saviour.

SUTTON: As I said, your Lord Jagannath is a piece of wood, a piece of neem wood—something to cook food with; something on which owls perch and hoot. Your god is so helpless that he can't save himself when you cut him up in little pieces or set him on fire.

VILLAGER: Hail Hari! Hail Krishna! This padre is bad-mouthing Lord Jagannath. Let's not stay here a minute longer.

VILLAGER I: Let's take the books and be off.

They tear the books from SUTTON*'s hand and go away. Enter* SUNDARDAS *accompanied by others.* SUTTON *shakes his hand and greets him.*

SUTTON: Welcome Sundardas. I was telling these people about the Puri temple.

SUNDARDAS: Oh, that temple is a den of vice.

SUTTON: Sadhu Sundardas, I beg you to enlighten these people about it.

SUNDARDAS: I have nothing to tell them, but I have something to tell you. You have a responsibility in this regard. In fact, I have addressed a letter to all Christians which I might as well read aloud. (*Takes out a letter and reads it.*) O ye favoured people, who are blessed with the divine spirit, ye have existed 1800 years, and what have you done for this dark world? I am a Hindu Boistub, poor and destitute, but ask you neither land, nor elephants, nor horses, nor money, nor palanquins, nor doolies; but I ask, what can be

done to teach the people to obey the laws of God. O holy people this I ask. Puri is the heaven of the Hindus; yet there the practices of mankind are adultery, theft, lies, murder of the innocent, whoremongery, eating fish with mahaprasad, disobedience and abuse of parents, defiling of mothers, defiling of sisters, defiling of daughters. Such is the religion of Jagannath. For these crimes, the people are visited with rheumatism, swellings of the legs, leprosy, scrofula, grievous sores, and acute pains, blindness, lameness, and such like. Such are the servants of Jagannath. And now holy people hear the names of the gods of this people—gods which the people, when they have eaten rice and worship—these are gold, silver, brass, cedar, stone, wood, trees, fire, water etc, these be the names of their gods, and these be their servants. To serve these gods, they burden themselves with expensive ceremonies and costly rites; they afflict their bodies, and their souls with pilgrimages and many cruelties. The Brahmuns no longer observe the Vedas, nor the devotees keep mercy. O ye Christian rulers, ye feed the rich, the proud and the great; while the poor and the destitute are dying in want. O good fathers; good children, good people, hear the cries of the poor, O good people.
The thief is judged, the murderer is judged, the perjurer is judged, and all the wicked are punished according to their crimes. A large army is kept in obedience to your orders. But why are not the people made to obey the laws of God? Ye are the seed of the good, ye keep God's word.

Exit SUNDARDAS. SUTTON *tries to follow him, but* SUNDARDAS *turns to forbid him and vanishes. A little later the* VILLAGERS *gather.* SUTTON *seems to receive a new surge of enthusiasm.*

SUTTON: Brothers and sisters, here, take these books. They are being given away for free. The Gospel according to St Luke, the Gospel according to St Mathew, the Gospel according to St Mark, the Gospel according to St John, the Sermon on the Mount, the Ten Commandments, the Book of Catechism, the Holy Bible.

No one shows any interest. SUTTON *tries to press the books on them.*

VILLAGERS: We don't want them, we won't take them.
SUTTON: Free, free! No money.
VILLAGERS: We won't take them even if you pay us.
VILLAGER: He's out to rob us of our caste and religion by giving us printed paper for free.
VILLAGER: They've put a hex on their printed books; we must not touch them. (*Turns to* SUTTON.) We have our palm-leaf scriptures, thank you very much. We don't need yours.
VILLAGERS: (*Among themselves.*) Run, folks, run. If we accept the padre's books we'll have no choice; we'll be under his spell.

The VILLAGERS *scatter in all directions, without taking the books.* SUTTON, *surprised, stands rooted to the ground.*

Scene IV

BAMPTON *is seen preaching to a crowd on a village road.*

BAMPTON: Brothers, I've come to show you the path to salvation, how to avoid hell. Hell is full of fire, sulphur and brimstone. The Holy Book says that sinners will be sent to hell. All human beings are sinners; but there is hope nevertheless. Listen carefully. There's only one god, and he loves all human beings. Even Hindus. He has a son, whose name is Jesus Christ. Jesus was originally with god in heaven, but god loved the earth so much that he sent his son down to save the human race, so that they wouldn't be destroyed but attain eternal life instead. Jesus Christ sacrificed himself for our sins; he gave up his life for us. If we put our faith in him, his blood will cleanse us of sin. That is the only path to salvation; there is no other. There is no other saviour. Learn about him and attain heaven.

BAMPTON *distributes the books.* VILLAGERS *chant 'Hail Hari' and disrupt the distribution before leaving en masse.* IRUN *stays behind. When* BAMPTON *leaves, he follows him.*

BAMPTON: Why are you following me?
IRUN: Padre sir, I want to become a Christian.
BAMPTON: Are you mocking me?
IRUN: (*Touches his ears.*) No sir!
BAMPTON: What's your name?
IRUN: Irun Senapati.
BAMPTON: If you wish to become a Christian, first wipe the holy ash off your forehead.

IRUN *wipes his forehead.* BAMPTON *helps him.*

BAMPTON: Now throw away the charm you're wearing.
IRUN: (*Fingers the charm.*) It's made of silver, sir.
BAMPTON: Unless you throw it away, I won't convert you.

IRUN *breaks it into pieces and offers them to* BAMPTON.

IRUN: There. Take the pieces.
BAMPTON: Now you have cast off your old religion.
IRUN: If you say so. But if someone asks you whether I have eaten in your place, please deny it even if it were true.
BAMPTON: I never tell lies. Where can I find some water?
IRUN: Ramalinga Pond is nearby.
BAMPTON: Let's go there.

Exit BAMPTON *and* IRUN. *The pond.*

BAMPTON: Do you worship Hindu gods?
IRUN: No.
BAMPTON: What, you don't?
IRUN: No sir.

BAMPTON: What is your opinion about Hindu scriptures?
IRUN: They're all false.
BAMPTON: You are a sinner.
IRUN: Maybe so.
BAMPTON: Who saves sinners?
IRUN: Who?
BAMPTON: Jesus Christ. And what did he do to save sinners?
IRUN: I remember what you said: He gave up his life to save sinners.
BAMPTON: Who shall be saved?
IRUN: He who believes in Jesus Christ.
BAMPTON: Do you believe in Jesus Christ?
IRUN: Yes sir.
BAMPTON: Will you follow his teachings?
IRUN: Yes sir.
BAMPTON: Jesus Christ said not to work on the Sabbath. Will you obey him?
IRUN: Gladly, sir. Who wants to work?
BAMPTON: Are you ready to be baptised?
IRUN: What is that, sir?
BAMPTON: I will dunk you in water and baptise you.
IRUN: I will drown, sir. I don't know how to swim. And if I die my two wives will die too.
BAMPTON: Let's get into the water.

BAMPTON *pushes* IRUN'*s head under water.*

BAMPTON: I baptise you in the name of the Father, the Son and the Holy Ghost.
IRUN: Very well.
BAMPTON: You are the first Oriya to convert. The first Christian of Orissa.
IRUN: I am not Oriya, sir. I'm Telugu.
BAMPTON: Telugu? Then we will have to look for an Oriya, the first Oriya Christian, the first success of the Orissa Baptist Mission. (*Thinks.*) Sundardas. Yes, he's the ideal choice.

IRUN: What am I to do now, sir?

BAMPTON: Will your people accept you, will they let you into your house?

IRUN: Never sir! I've lost my caste. Who will let me into the house?

BAMPTON: What was your caste?

IRUN: Weaver. Now it is god's caste.

BAMPTON: Now that you have become a Christian, what does that matter? What do you wish to do?

IRUN: I want to march straight into the Jagannath temple at Puri flanked by you and the king of Puri and challenge Him to produce His miracles. If He doesn't then I'll kick Him about a bit. That will show people that He counts for nothing.

BAMPTON: What else?

IRUN: Smash to pieces all the idols and statues all the world over.

BAMPTON: Very well. All that can wait. First come and have some tea with me.

Enter MADMAN.

MADMAN: Where is he? Where is the padre? Where is Jesus Christ? Where is god? Where is the horse? Oh, Lord God, our Father thou art in Heaven, I am a miserable sinner. The greatest sinner on earth; none worse than me. There are no depths to my depravity; I deserve to go to Hell.

Enter some VILLAGERS, *looking for* MADMAN.

VILLAGER: There you are!

MADMAN: Oh Lord, you are the saviour of the helpless, you sent your son Jesus Christ to save the miserable and the wretched of the earth. He shed his precious blood to save sinners. It is to him that I pray to save my soul, to rid me of my sins.

MADMAN *holds* BAMPTON *in a tight embrace.*

BAMPTON: Let go.

MADMAN: Never. I will never let go of you, I will cling to you. I will pray to my new god, I will become a devotee of Jesus Christ.

VILLAGER: What did you say, you wretch? Become a Christian, will you? Eat beef? Drink wine? Sleep with Firinghee women? Sick of the Hindu religion already, is that right? Just because you can't do any of those things, huh?

MADMAN: Oh Jagannath, Radhakrushna, Rama, Govinda, Keshab, Daitari, Mahadev, Chandi, Chamundi, Bhairav, Ganesh; oh Kali, Bagala, Chhinnamasta, Bhubaneswari, Matangini, Sodashi, Dhumawati, Tripurasundari, Bhairavi; oh thirty-three million thousand gods, oh ten incarnations of Vishnu; oh gurus, Brahmins, idols and deities; oh mantras, yantras, vedas, vedantas, Bhagavat, Ramayan, Parayan, Narayan; oh Kasi, Vrindavan, Dwarka, Ganga; oh matted hair, holy marks across the forehead, rites and rituals, festivals and worship, consecrated prasad and mahaprasad—everything is false.

VILLAGER: (*Beats* MADMAN.) What did you say—all false? What is true then, you wretch?

MADMAN: Our Father, thou art in Heaven, Jesus Christ, padre, horse. They are all true.

VILLAGER *slaps* MADMAN. BAMPTON *and* IRUN *try to stop him.*

VILLAGER: If you become a Christian, what will become of your wife and children? (*Pause.*) Fearing you might try to run away, we gave you a drink spiked with dhatura, but nothing seems to have any effect. We took you to the goddess at Jajpur, paid the Brahmin priests to say prayers for you, had the scriptures read out loud, but nothing has made any impression. What you really need is a sound thrashing.

MADMAN: (*Sings.*) The love of Jesus Christ is without parallel; there is nothing like it anywhere.

VILLAGER: Shut up. Sing from the Bhagavat.

MADMAN: Not from the Bhagavat.

VILLAGER *beats him.*

MADMAN: Stop it, stop it. I'm willing to sing from the Bhagavat.
Hail Nrushingha, holy thou art,
Thou art the cause of it all,
Thou art without beginning,
Without middle and end,
Nothing moves without your command.
Thou created the senses,
Thou art the Truth.

MADMAN *grabs* BAMPTON *once again.*

MADMAN:
Lucky is he who is Christian
He is a king without a throne
Lord God is his father and protector
Jesus Christ is his brother and saviour.

The VILLAGERS *pull him from* BAMPTON. BAMPTON *and* IRUN *pull him towards them. Pulled from* both *sides,* MADMAN *continues to sing.*

MADMAN: Listen, oh you King Parikshita, listen to the legends of Lord Krishna.

BAMPTON *and* IRUN *succeed in pulling* MADMAN *towards them.*

MADMAN: Listen, oh almighty King Parikshita, listen to the legends of Jesus Christ, listen to the Bible.

MADMAN, *pulled to and fro, falls to the ground.* VILLAGER *picks him up quickly and drags him away.* BAMPTON *mutters under his breath: 'Sundardas', as if the holy man of Kujibar could provide the solution.*

Scene V

LACEY *and* SUTTON *are in the middle of a discussion in the street.*

LACEY: It's been nearly six years since we set up the Mission in Orissa, but we're yet to convert a single Oriya. Irun Senapati doesn't count; he's a Telugu.

SUTTON: I had set high hopes on Sundardas; I thought he would be our first Oriya convert, but he's proved elusive.

LACEY *puts his finger to his lips signalling for silence. They both look up the street and see* SUNDARDAS *walking away in the distance. They follow him.* SUNDARDAS *looks over his shoulder and gestures to them not to follow, but the padres do nevertheless.* SUNDARDAS *vanishes in the blink of an eye. In his place the padres see* GANGADHAR. *They hurry and catch up to him.*

LACEY: (*To* GANGADHAR.) Well, have you made up your mind?

GANGADHAR: It's been made up for a long time. The only problem is that my relatives have been threatening me.

SUTTON: Cut yourself off from your relatives.

GANGADHAR: I would, but they won't.

Enter the VILLAGERS.

VILLAGERS: Look, look, Brother Gangadhar is here. The padres have done a good job of keeping him from us.

LACEY: (*To* GANGADHAR.) Tell them what you've decided.

GANGADHAR: Yes, it's time that I did.

VILLAGERS: Enough is enough, Brother Gangadhar, it's time you returned home. How long will you eat the crumbs, the leftovers from the padres' table?

GANGADHAR: Listen to me, please. You've known me since I was a child. You know how I've always hungered for enlightenment. I read our scriptures, observed fasts and vigils, spent a good deal of time in worship. I pestered every Brahmin and sadhu I came across to share true knowledge with me, but their only advice was penance and more penance, worship and more worship. No one could tell me how to get rid of sin, how to escape hell. I was advised to go to the Jagannath temple. I went and offered prayers. But to no avail. Once while I was going around Lord Jagannath on his diamond-studded throne I even stuck a needle into Him, but nothing happened. Then I finally landed in Kujibar ashram, and it was Sundara Baba who opened my eyes. It was he who explained to me that gods and goddesses are all false, that the caste system is evil. It was there that I read with him the books handed out by the padres, and saw the light. It was the Bible that finally saved me. When I read about Jesus Christ, it struck me that I was one of the sinners for whom Jesus had laid down his life. I began to pray to him to give me strength to keep my faith unwavering until I die. I've decided to receive baptism and become a Christian.

VILLAGER: All right, but come with us to the village first. We have all the time in the world to discuss your conversion.

GANGADHAR: No. I won't go with you until I've been baptised.

VILLAGERS: We refuse to leave without you.

LACEY: (*To the* VILLAGERS.) I'm taking Gangadhar to the Mahanadi river to be baptised. You may return to your village.

GANGADHAR *and* LACEY *proceed to the river and down the bank into the water. The* VILLAGERS *crowd around them.*

LACEY: (*To* GANGADHAR.) Do you believe in god?

GANGADHAR: Yes.

LACEY: But Hindus speak of many gods—Brahma, Vishnu, Maheswar, and a host of others besides!

GANGADHAR: They are all false gods.

LACEY: Will you give them up?

GANGADHAR: Yes.
LACEY: What about the charm you wear around your neck?

GANGADHAR *tears off the string of basil beads and hands it to the padre.*

LACEY: Are you ready to repent?
GANGADHAR: Yes.
LACEY: Do you believe in Jesus Christ for your redemption?
GANGADHAR: Yes.
LACEY: Will you obey Christ's teachings until you die?
GANGADHAR: Yes sir, I will.

LACEY *dunks* GANGADHAR *in the water.*

LACEY: I baptise you in the name of God the father, God the Son and the Holy Ghost.
GANGADHAR: Very well.

The VILLAGERS *shout Hail Hari and discuss* GANGADHAR*'s conversion; they leave, threatening him.*

VILLAGERS: All right. We're going back. But remember, from this moment you have been ostracised. You can't obtain water or fire from anyone in the village. You'd better stay away, if you value your life. If you set foot in the village you might be stoned to death.

SUTTON, LACEY *and* GANGADHAR *notice* SUNDARDAS *in the distance and run after him.* SUNDARDAS *looks over his shoulder and gestures not to follow him, but they persist.* SUNDARDAS *vanishes in the twinkling of an eye, and in his place is* RAMACHANDRA. *They catch hold of him. Enter soon afterwards* RAMACHANDRA*'s wife, his elderly mother, his children and some people from his village. They surround the padres,* GANGADHAR, *and* RAMACHANDRA.

RAMACHANDRA'S MOTHER: (*To* RAMACHANDRA.) Did I carry you in my womb for nine months to see this? Why didn't you die the moment you were born?
RAMACHANDRA'S WIFE: Are you under the spell of some witch?
RAMACHANDRA'S SON: Father, if you become a Christian, I will hang myself.
VILLAGERS: RAMACHANDRA, look at Barabati Fort, where your father was once the chief. As the son of such an illustrious person, how can you be so eager to become a padre's slave? Better to die than to blacken the faces of the Hindus!

Silence.

VILLAGERS: Better to take to begging or to performing the duties of the low-castes than to convert to Christianity! You're no longer part of the community. We don't want to see your face any longer. Let's go, let the unfortunate dog stay back to scour for the scraps off the padre's table.

They try to pull RAMACHANDRA *away, but he resists. Exit* VILLAGERS. SUTTON *and* LACEY *lead* RAMACHANDRA *into the river for his baptism.*

LACEY: Do you wish to embrace Christianity?
RAMACHANDRA: Yes.
SUTTON: Why?
RAMACHANDRA: Because I believe in Christ.
LACEY: How deeply do you believe in Christ?
RAMACHANDRA: With all my heart and soul.
SUTTON: Do believers remain in sin?
RAMACHANDRA: No.
LACEY: Do you sin by telling lies, uttering vile curses, shouting at people?
RAMACHANDRA: No longer. I've given all that up.
SUTTON: You once worshipped idols?

RAMACHANDRA: Yes.
LACEY: Do you still?
RAMACHANDRA: No, no longer. I swept all the idols into a cloth bundle and tied it to the ceiling and threw dirt on it; some idols broke, the rest I set fire to.
SUTTON: Have you consulted anyone about your conversion?
RAMACHANDRA: My own people. The villagers too. They were all up in arms against the idea. I consulted Gangadhar, and he was encouraging. I spoke to Sundara Baba, but he put me off.
LACEY: Are you still willing to convert?
RAMACHANDRA: yes.

LACEY *baptises* RAMACHANDRA.

LACEY: I baptise you in the name of God the Father, God the Son and the Holy Ghost.
RAMACHANDRA: Very well.

They notice SUNDARDAS *in the distance and follow him.* SUNDARDAS *looks over his shoulder to forbid them, but they do not take heed.* SUNDARDAS *vanishes suddenly, and in his place is* KRUPASINDHU SAHU. *They drag* KRUPASINDHU *into the water.*

SUTTON: (*To* KRUPASINDHU.) Do you believe in the Hindu gods?
KRUPASINDHU: No.
LACEY: What about Hindu scriptures?
KRUPASINDHU: They're all false.
SUTTON: Are you a sinner?
KRUPASINDHU: Yes, I am.
LACEY: Who redeems sinners?
KRUPASINDHU: Jesus Christ.
SUTTON: What did he do for sinners?
KRUPASINDHU: He gave up his life.

LACEY: Who shall be redeemed?
KRUPASINDHU: Those who believe in Jesus Christ.
SUTTON: Do you believe in Jesus Christ?
KRUPASINDHU: Yes.
LACEY: Are you ready for baptism?
KRUPASINDHU: Yes.

SUTTON *baptises* KRUPASINDHU.

SUTTON: I baptise you in the name of God the Father, God the Son and the Holy Ghost.
KRUPASINDHU: Very well.

They notice SUNDARDAS *in the distance and run after him.* SUNDARDAS *looks over his shoulder and signals for them not to follow, but they do not pay attention. Suddenly* SUNDARDAS *vanishes, and in his place are* KAMALI *with her ten-month-old baby at her breast, and her mother,* DAANI. *The padres drag them to the river. They clearly hear* SUNDARDAS *say: 'No!' but they do continue on.*

KAMALI: I want to become a Christian.
DAANI: Yes sir. Convert both me and my daughter.
GANGADHAR: You have been to Sundara Baba, no? How did he react to the idea?
KAMALI: He told us not to convert, to go back to our homes, but we decided to come here anyway.
DAANI: Our menfolk were away when we left home.
KAMALI: I left my elder daughter with a neighbour and brought this little child along; she's still to be weaned.
DAANI: Please convert us without delay. If our men turn up here before the conversion, they will make trouble.
LACEY: Have you made up your minds?
KAMALI: Absolutely. We wish to become Christians.
DAANI: We are sinners. Our own gods could do nothing to save us. Only Christ can save us.

Enter VILLAGERS, *among them the husbands of* KAMALI *and* DAANI. *There is commotion.*

KAMALI'S HUSBAND: How dare you leave home on your own? Have you forgotten you're a woman? Come with me, let's go back.

KAMALI: We have come here to become Christians.

DAANI'S HUSBAND: What, have you taken leave of your senses? Where's your modesty, your manners? How could two women leave the village on their own and venture into town? Come on, come back home. You have to be purified.

DAANI: Not before we embrace Christianity.

KAMALI'S HUSBAND: Forget it. We won't let you do any such mad thing.

VILLAGERS: This bloody padre has addled their brains. Before they concentrated on converting men, now they are after women as well. Who'd have imagined the day would come when docile Hindu women would boldly leave home to become Christians!

LACEY: I'm not forcing them to convert. You're free to persuade them to go back home with you. They're welcome to leave.

VILLAGERS *try to persuade* KAMALI *and* DAANI, *but fail.* KAMALI *and* DAANI *remain steadfast in their resolve.*

DAANI'S HUSBAND: (*To* VILLAGERS.) Let's go back. Leave the women alone. We shouldn't even look at sinners like them for too long.

KAMALI'S HUSBAND: These two wretched women have crossed over to the side of the Firinghees and lost their dignity, chastity and character. All relations with them are broken off as of this moment.

DAANI'S HUSBAND: It's as if they had died. We must hurry home and observe the funeral rites. Come, let's get a move on. No point in witnessing this transgression.

Exit VILLAGERS. SUTTON *and* LACEY *wade into the water with* KAMALI *and* DAANI.

LACEY: (*To* KAMALI.) Are you ready for baptism?
KAMALI: Yes.

SUNDARDAS'*s voice is heard from afar: 'No!'*

SUTTON: (*To* DAANI.) You are sure you want to be baptised?
DAANI: Yes.

Again SUNDARDAS'*s voice is heard: 'No!'* SUTTON *and* LACEY *baptise the two women.*

SUTTON: (*To* DAANI.) I baptise you in the name of God the father, God the Son and the Holy Ghost.
LACEY: (*To* KAMALI.) I baptise you in the name of God the father, God the Son and the Holy Ghost.
DAANI: Very well.
KAMALI: Very well.

SUNDARDAS'*s voice is heard from afar: 'No, no, no!'*

ACT THREE

Scene I

Three years later. CHARLES LACEY'*s house in Cuttack.* LACEY's *wife,* ANN, *assisted by* MARUA, *is tidying up the drawing room.*

ANN: Mary, is everything ready for the tea?
MARUA: Yes, Sister.
ANN: We're expecting quite a few guests.
MARUA: Brother Lacey's certainly taking a long time to get back home.
ANN: He went to the chapel. He should be here any moment now.
MARUA: Who is coming to tea, Sister?
ANN: Brother Sutton from Balasore; Brother Bampton from Puri, he's been in town for two days already; and Brother Pears of the Christian Missionary Herald. Have the cups and plates been washed and wiped?
MARUA: (*Lays the table.*) Yes, Sister. Everything's ready.
ANN: I'll see to the tea. You tidy up the table and arrange the cutlery.

Exit ANN.

MARUA: Where are the forks? These people have hands just like everyone else but when it comes to eating they ask for forks! David! (*Getting no reply, in a raised voice.*) David!

BALABHADRA *steals in silently. He is wearing pants and a shirt.*

MARUA: Have you gone deaf or something? I must have shouted your name ten times!
BALABHADRA: What am I to do if people keep changing my

name? How many names can I remember? In the village it was Balia. The Kondhs called me Meria. Sundara Baba changed it to Balabhadra. And here I'm called David.

MARUA: So what? I was Marua in the village, but Mary here. Call me Marua and I say, yes; call me Mary and I say, yes sir; if some one calls me Darling, I will say, yes dear!

BALABHADRA: Listen Marua, I'm planning to run away.

MARUA: Do what you want, but first arrange the forks on the table. I can see that you're not the kind to settle down anywhere.

BALABHADRA: (*Fiddling with the forks.*) The forks are right under your nose. Can't you see them? Not only have you lost your faith by living with the Firinghees, you've lost your eyesight too. Why don't you become a Christian and be done with it? That Christian cook Abraham is mad about you.

MARUA: Abraham's no longer a cook. Didn't you know? That smart Bengali boy has picked up Oriya so well that the padres have pressed him into preaching. Guess what his salary is—seven rupees a month! But look at you—you've lived here for a long time but are still the dimwit you were before, no improvement at all.

BALABHADRA: Look, I may not have gone to school, but I'm no fool. I can tell you all about Creation if you want. In the beginning God created the heaven and the earth. And the earth was without form and void; and darkness was upon the face of the deep. And the Spirit of God moved upon the face of the waters. And God said, Let there be light: and there was light. Do you understand, Marua, Mary?

MARUA: Yes sir, Balia, Meria, Balabhadra, David! But I don't need to know about their Creation. Let the devils have their own ideas. I want nothing to do with them, and nothing to do with their religion either. Let Sundara Baba and Padre Lacey worry about that. All that matters to me is that I have to work, earn my wages, live out the rest of my days, that's all. If in the midst of it all you happen to get a smile and a kind word from someone, consider yourself lucky.

BALABHADRA: You talk as if you were better off in the village!

MARUA: Women's fate is always the same, whether we're in the village or the town. In the village the rich and the Brahmins are after us; here it is the Firinghees. What difference does it make?

BALABHADRA: Why don't you become a Christian?

MARUA: How did conversion help Kamali and her mother? It was like going from the frying pan into the fire. Their husbands threw them out, and now they're on the street.

BALABHADRA: Bloody hell. It'd be a lot better if there was no religion at all. Look, I don't have a religion. My father was very religious, but he sold me off for a few filthy coins. The Kondhs fed and fattened me so that I'd make a good sacrifice. Then I came to the ashram where there was no god but a hundred and one dos and don'ts. And now I am with these Firinghee mlechhas. What religion do I have?

MARUA: Be happy then.

BALABHADRA: But how? Is this my home? Was the ashram my home? Or the Kondh village? My home is in my village, where I was plain Balia—not Balabhadra, not David. I'm always thinking about my village. What about you, do you ever think about yours?

MARUA: A woman doesn't belong anywhere. Wherever she lives is her village. Whoever takes her is her husband, lord and master; wherever he takes her is her home. Understand? Take Ann memsahib. Just because she married the padre she's crossed seven seas to set up home here. And mind you all she does is offer tea to the padre's guests. Now get on with the work, boy, and get the table ready.

Enter LACEY, SUTTON, GANGADHAR, RADHU DAS. *They proceed to the table.*

SUTTON: With all those trees and shrubs the chapel looks beautiful.

RADHU DAS: It is a holy place. The Hindus always choose fine sites for their temples.

SUTTON: The first church in Orissa has been built on the ruins of a temple—that's a good sign.

RAGHU: A good sign? The Muslims razed Hindu temples and built mosques on the same site. Now the Christians are doing the same thing with their churches.

LACEY: But the Shiva temple was already in ruins and nobody ever offered prayers there. Isn't it a good thing that a place of worship has been built there, so what if it's a church?

SUTTON: A place of true worship where once was a den of heathen practices. Monstrous idols replaced by the living Jesus Christ; the cacophony of primitive rituals replaced by quietude and sibilant prayers to God and the Lamb.

LACEY: The light from the church will illuminate the whole of Orissa.

SUTTON: May the time come soon when there will be only churches and no temples. All heathen temples should be razed to the ground.

LACEY: That will be a wonderful day for Orissa.

SUTTON: When I looked at the chapel this morning, I couldn't help but love this land of Orissa. There's everything here: fertile soil, dense forests, green hills, full rivers, everything. If only Oriyas would take to the Bible, this place would become paradise on earth. It would yield gold, it would turn into the land of Emmanuel. It would be full of places of living worship; but instead of temples there would be churches everywhere. It would be full of blessed folks, all worshipping the one true God; its roads would be teeming with pilgrims and they would all be seekers of the true faith. The only scripture would be the Holy Bible. There would be songs on the lips of its people but those will be the joyous prayers extolling God and the Lamb. All Oriya parents would become true Christians and observe the Sabbath.

LACEY: (*Flips open the Bible and reads.*) The wilderness and the solitary place shall be glad for them; and the desert shall rejoice, and blossom as the rose. It will blossom abundantly, and rejoice even with joy and singing: the glory of Lebanon shall be given unto it, the excellency of Carmel and Sharon, they shall see the glory of the Lord, and the excellency of our God.

SUTTON: Amen.

LACEY: Once, a long time ago, when I was walking down a road, I sat down on a Hindu idol and asked my servant to find out what passers-by thought about that. He reported that they said only a Firinghee sahib could do this, for he was so strong that he feared no one.

RAGHU: Does that mean you will raze our temples to the ground?

RADHU DAS: Brother, why are you obsessed with that idea? Where was your temple here?

RAGHU: Have you forgotten that there was a Shiva temple on the very site where the church now stands?

RADHU DAS: Aeons ago. All we ever saw was rubble. The place was a wilderness, crawling with snakes, jackals and other beasts. Did anybody ever visit the deity or offer worship?

RAGHU: No matter. I'm not going to sell away my piece of land. My land houses a holy Hanuman temple.

RADHU DAS: What Hanuman temple? Where? There's only a stone image of Hanuman under the open sky exposed to the elements.

RAGHU: For us the temple is wherever there's an idol.

RADHU DAS: But is the idol being worshipped?

RAGHU: Not being worshipped doesn't make any difference to a god. Worship can resume at any moment. Anyway, haven't you noticed that the idol of Hanuman is dabbed with vermilion? Tell your padre I won't sell my land.

RADHU DAS: But I know you, Brahmin! If the price is right you'll readily sell your gods! So stop bluffing and tell us the price.

RAGHU: Sorry, the land is not for sale.

RADHU DAS: (*To* LACEY.) He says he won't sell the land. (*To* RAGHU.) Then you may leave, Brahmin. (RAGHU *does not budge.*) All right, now get a move on. There's no point sitting here. Surely you won't take tea and biscuits in a Firinghee mlechha's home, will you?

RAGHU: But who's talking to you?

LACEY: So what's your best price?

RAGHU: (*Looks at* RADHU DAS, *but speaks to* LACEY.) I will come some other time. We need to talk one to one.

LACEY: No need for further discussion, if you're unwilling to sell the land.

RAGHU: I never said I was unwilling. All I said was I'd never sell the statue of Lord Hanuman. Our gods are not for sale, no matter how high the price.

Exit RAGHU.

LACEY: Radhu Das, what do you think—will he sell his land?

RADHU DAS: Sir, I know him better than the back of my hand. Take it from me that the sale is already decided. The only thing that remains to be sorted out is the price.

LACEY: We badly need that piece of land because it adjoins the chapel. If we have it, we'll build a house for Gangadhar on it. The poor man lost his house and land by becoming a Christian. Besides, it will be of immense help if he lives nearby. (*To* GANGADHAR.) What do you say, Gangadhar?

GANGADHAR: That would be fine.

SUTTON: What about paying a visit to Saint Sundardas and convincing him?

GANGADHAR: I've been visiting him off and on, but lately he's been barely civil to me. He's upset over our conversion. He's angry with everyone—Ramachandra, Krupasindhu, everyone. He flew into a towering rage when he heard that Kamali and her mother had converted against their husband's wishes.

SUTTON: But we didn't force anyone into Christianity! Each one of you was a willing convert. We preach, and those who come to us do so on their own.

Enter the VILLAGERS, *followed by* BAMPTON. *For once the padre is dressed in his regular gear, he is even wearing shoes. Between persistent coughings he sings a psalm.*

BAMPTON: I was out preaching at Chandini Chowk this morning but could hardly get going. (*Coughs.*) I can't stop coughing. I hadn't brought enough books for the people there, so these have followed me back to get their copies.

LACEY *gets some books and distributes them.*

BAMPTON: Brother Lacey, I'm not in a position to preach. (*Breaks into a spell of coughing.*) Please tell these brothers a little about Jesus Christ.

The VILLAGERS *squat down on the floor, ready to listen.*

LACEY: Brothers, I'll begin with the birth of Jesus Christ. (*He opens the Bible and reads from it.*) Now the birth of Jesus Christ was on this wise: When as his mother Mary was espoused to Joseph, before they came together . . .

From the back MARUA *stifles an urge to vomit. LACEY turns pale. Everyone is taken by surprise. After a few moments of tense silence, Lacey raises his voice unnaturally high and plods on.*

LACEY: She was found with the child of Holy Ghost. Then Joseph her husband being just *man*, and not willing to make her a public example, was minded to put her away privily. But while he thought on these things, behold, the angel of the Lord appeared unto him in a dream, saying, Joseph, thou son of David, fear not to take unto thee Mary thy wife: for that which is conceived in her is of the Holy Ghost.

LACEY *stops for breath.* MARUA *is still being sick.*

BAMPTON: Patience, Mary. I'll give you some medicine. (*Coughs.*)
MARUA: It must be the fish I ate last night; it wasn't fresh.

LACEY *heaves a sigh of relief.* BAMPTON *coughs.*

LACEY: (*To the* VILLAGERS.) I'll tell you how Jesus Christ fed five hundred people with just a few fish.

VILLAGERS: Don't bother. We've heard enough already, and seen enough too. Now we'll read these books and find out for ourselves.

Exit the VILLAGERS.

SUTTON: Brother Bampton, please don't keep singing that song. I'll write you a new one.

BAMPTON: Sorry, Brother Sutton. It just happens to be my favourite. (*Coughs.*) Please don't ever ask me to stop singing it.

SUTTON: But Brother, I'll write you a proper Oriya song. I might not be as good in Oriya as you or Brother Lacey are—well, blame it on my voice and accent—but I've studied the language quite thoroughly. It's a rich language and has more ancient texts than might be imagined; unfortunately, they all deal with the Hindu religion one way or another. I'm currently at work on Oriya grammar.

BAMPTON: (*Despite rising waves of coughing.*) I find the old song good enough. Brother Carey taught it to us at Serampore. His native accountant penned it in praise of Jesus Christ.

SUTTON: Strange that Carey's accountant, who was a die-hard Hindu, and who resisted all attempts at conversion, should have written such a wonderful prayer.

LACEY: I think the fellow was something like our Sundardas.

GANGADHAR: But don't cherish any hopes of Baba ever consenting to convert.

LACEY: What did he tell you when you met him last?

GANGADHAR: He said he'd drop in one of these days to have it out with you. He' s no longer his old self; he's a changed man. After Kamali's and her mother's baptism he has no kind words for you; in fact, he denounces you.

SUTTON: What a strange land! Anybody's free to convert out of his or her own free will. Why should anyone take umbrage at that?

LACEY: Ramachandra's wife left him after his conversion, but now she's back with him.

They notice that BAMPTON *has fallen asleep.* SUTTON *rouses him and he wakes up with a start and asks for his horse. Everyone laughs.*

SUTTON: The only thought Brother Bampton has on his mind is to ride from one place to another and preach.

LACEY: Wherever he finds a marketplace, a temple, a bazar, a fair, or a village on his way, he dismounts and begins to preach the word of the Lord.

BAMPTON: (*In a fit of coughing.*) I'm not doing too well. I find it increasingly tiring to ride a horse.

LACEY: You'll be all right soon.

From outside the sound of a palanquin being lowered on the ground. Enter PEARS.

LACEY: Welcome, Brother Pears!

They all greet him. Enter ANN. *She and* PEARS *shake hands and ask after each other's welfare.* ANN *and* MARUA *serve tea.*

PEARS: I didn't realize the Puri road was so bad. The trip took a long time. The visit was a waste of time because Brother Bampton had already left for Cuttack.

BAMPTON *who has fallen asleep again is awakened by* LACEY.

BAMPTON: (*Waking up with a start.*) And Jesus came and spake unto them, saying, All power is given unto me in heaven and in earth. Go ye therefore, and teach all nations, baptizing them in the name of the Father, of the Son, and the Holy Ghost: Teaching them to observe all things whatsoever I have commanded you: and lo, I am with you always, even unto the end of the world. Amen.

PEARS: Wonderful, Brother Bampton! You're exactly like what I'd heard about you. But I had expected to see you in native dress.

BAMPTON: When I first came to work in Orissa I thought shame upon me as a padre, and as an Englishman too, if I cannot dress and behave like a Hindu native, so I gave up wearing shoes and wore only a dhoti and a vest. It's a lot easier to negotiate the mud and puddles dressed like that than in our Western clothes. The natives too took to me because of how I was dressed, but soon I realised that it did me no good; they were only laughing at me. My feet bled and I found it hard to walk about. The leeches got at me freely. So in the end I had to stop dressing like a native.

PEARS: You're not too well. Why don't you move to Cuttack? Sticking to Puri is not going to do you any good.

BAMPTON: The whole of Orissa is a land of heathens and Puri is the centre of their evil empire. So I decided to live right there. I thought preaching in front of the Jagannath temple would be like pulling at the lion's whiskers in its own den!

PEARS: But there's not a single convert to show for all that.

BAMPTON: Brother, you have to be patient and cautious in a place like Puri. If a big fly is trapped in the web, the spider does not attack immediately. You have to have patience in addition to cunning. If you're too hasty, the quarry might flee.

PEARS: Are you referring to Sundardas, by any chance? I've heard about him.

BAMPTON: No, I'm talking about the natives of Puri. A wily lot they are. Meanwhile I've gone and met the king of Puri and spoken to him about Jesus Christ and given him the tracts. A few temple priests too have stopped by to hear me preach. I have every hope and confidence that sooner rather than later I'll be able to baptise a few.

PEARS: There hasn't exactly been a flood of conversions outside Puri either.

SUTTON: There might not be many conversions here in Orissa, but it's unlike anywhere else in the country. Here the converts are all from the high castes, and they've taken to Christianity because they love and believe in Jesus Christ. Elsewhere it's the low-caste and uneducated people who have converted, mostly in the hope of bettering their lot or landing a job. Take our first convert Gangadhar. A blue-blooded Brahmin if there was one, and a pundit who's well-versed in the scriptures. He converted because he felt Christianity was the better religion. Another thing. None of the converts in Orissa have left the fold.

PEARS: Now, that's really something.

LACEY: Yes, as Brother Sutton said, all our Oriya converts are from the higher castes, from the upper class. There are Brahmins and Karans, teachers and astrologers. Not one person became a Christian out of greed or because of other inducements. On the contrary, they've all suffered. Not only did they lose their old religion and caste, they lost their homes and lands, jobs and families as well.

PEARS: But what's the problem with converting Sundardas?

LACEY: He simply hasn't been converted, but we're still hopeful. He doesn't worship idols, he believes in the Ten Commandments, he reads and appreciates the Gospels. Some of his close disciples have already converted. So it's really only a matter of time. Of course it will be our crowning glory when we get Sundardas to convert.

PEARS: What problems do you face when you go out to preach?

LACEY: The biggest is the Company—its laws and its officers. The Company pays money to the Jagannath temple; the pilgrim tax goes to temple maintenance. Naturally the Hindus keep raising the issue: if the Jagannath temple is nothing, why is the Company collecting a pilgrim tax and handing it over to the temple?

BAMPTON: Mind you, I keep telling them that the pilgrim tax is actually nothing but a fine for idol worship!

SUTTON: The Company's magistrates are against us. They're angry with us because of our open criticism of the pilgrim tax. If it were abolished, they'd lose their jobs.

BAMPTON: They're hardly ever just, either. My servants tried to poison my wife, but the magistrate set them free.

LACEY: The Company laws and regulations are strange. If a male Hindu converts he forfeits his right to property and his Hindu wife can't be forced to live with him. All the converts here lost not only their homes and land but their families as well. So you can imagine the sacrifices people have made for the cause.

SUTTON: That apart, the Company collectors and magistrates and commanders have all taken to a life of sin with their native mistresses. Deplorable characters, no wonder the natives equate Christianity with low morals.

Inside, MARUA *vomits.* PEARS *pricks up his ears.*

LACEY: (*Suddenly, unthinkingly.*) Virgin Mary. I mean our maid Mary. Rotten fish.

PEARS *looks at him uncomprehendingly.*

PEARS: (*Closing his notebook.*) Glad to have met you all. Could I see your chapel?

LACEY: It's three years old already. When it started in November 1826, there were only twelve members in the congregation. Now we have quite a number. Come along, let me show you around the chapel.

PEARS: No, don't bother. My palanquin is just outside, and with your permission I'll take Brother Bampton along so we can discuss a few things on the way. But I'll visit you again before I go back to Calcutta.

Exit PEARS *and* BAMPTON. *Enter* SUNDARDAS *with a few disciples.* GANGADHAR *and* RADHU DAS *prostrate themselves before him. Unthinkingly, both* LACEY *and* SUTTON *do the same.* SUNDARDAS *picks them up, and all shake hands.*

SUNDARDAS: What a beautiful place. I've never been inside a sahib's home before.

LACEY: It's our good fortune to receive you. Please take a chair. (*To* MARUA.) Mary, bring tea for Sadhu Sundardas.

SUNDARDAS *sits down.* MARUA *brings tea and biscuits.*

SUNDARDAS: Marua—Mary. Mary—Marua. Nice name. (*To* MARUA.) God bless you.

LACEY: Surely you don't have any objection to having tea in our home?

SUNDARDAS: But I don't take any intoxicants.

LACEY: Tea is not an intoxicant.

SUNDARDAS: No? Then why do you drink it? What are these other things?

MARUA: Biskuts.

SUNDARDAS: You mean poison cakes? (*He picks up one and examines it from all sides.*) If it's strictly vegetarian, I don't mind eating one. No, I don't have any objection to eating in a Firinghee home.

LACEY: Have no fear, these biscuits are completely vegetarian.

SUNDARDAS: (*Munching one.*) It tastes good.

SUTTON: You're an admirable person: you look down on idol worship, you believe in the Ten Commandments, you don't mind having food and water in our home.

SUNDARDAS: But I'd mind becoming a Christian.

LACEY: But why? You don't believe in Hinduism!

SUNDARDAS: That's not true. The fact is I don't reject any religion. I believe in all that is fair, just and true; it doesn't have anything to do with religion. I find your Ten Commandments admirable so I tell everyone to practice them.

SUTTON: You have always spoken against the evil aspects of Hinduism.

SUNDARDAS: What is bad is bad, no matter what the scriptures have to say. And when have I told people to practice all the tenets of Hinduism? My teachings are simple: speak the truth, lead a just life, et cetera. Hinduism might be full of abominable practices, but trying to convert others is not one of them. It does not denounce other religions as evil. I wonder what Gangadhar has gained by his conversion. (*Turns to* GANGADHAR.) Well,

Gangadhar, are you any better off? What are you able to do now that you couldn't when you were a Hindu?

SUTTON: Gangadhar has a mind of his own. He didn't convert blindly.

SUNDARDAS: What about Ramachandra and Krupasindhu?

LACEY: They weren't children; they weren't forced. They converted voluntarily.

SUNDARDAS: And now this ignorant fool Radhu Das is all set to convert, if I'm not mistaken!

LACEY: Well, if that's what he wishes.

SUNDARDAS: You've betrayed me. I gave you Gangadhar and Ramachandra to help you preach the Ten Commandments, but you went and converted them without even consulting me.

LACEY: We didn't force them to convert; they did so out of their own sweet will. They began to believe in Jesus Christ.

SUNDARDAS: Gangadhar, do you believe in Jesus Christ?

GANGADHAR: Yes.

SUNDARDAS: And you believe everything that's written about him? In his miracles? Making the blind see, turning water to wine, stopping storms, bringing the dead back to life—you consider all these true?

SUTTON: Of course these are all true! Every word written in the Holy Bible is true. How can there be any doubt? You too work miracles!

SUNDARDAS: (*Laughs.*) Miracles! Miracles! All right, here's one for you.

He plucks a flower out of the air and hands it to SUTTON. SUTTON *is amazed.* SUNDARDAS *slowly takes out another flower from the folds of his shawl so that everyone can see. This flower he hands to* LACEY.

SUTTON: Oh God!

SUNDARDAS: Now let me tell you the purpose of my visit. You converted Kamali and her mother without their husbands' consent. That was highly unfair.

MARUA *who has been listening silently all this time now comes forward.*

MARUA: Baba, why is it highly unfair? You've always said men and women are equal. You don't practice discrimination between the sexes in your ashram. Why should a husband's consent be needed before a woman converts? Did Gangadhar and Ramachandra need their wives' consent? Ramachandra's wife was dead set against his conversion, I remember.

SUNDARDAS: So you too want to convert, Marua?

MARUA: You haven't answered my question, Baba.

LACEY: Mary, go inside. Be quiet when men are having a discussion.

MARUA: When it comes to women, padres are just like other men. Women must always keep quiet. Hunh!

Exit MARUA.

SUNDARDAS: You converted Gangadhar, and I didn't say anything. You converted Ramachandra and I still kept quiet. Then you converted Krupasindhu, but I chose to ignore it. But the conversion of Kamali and Daani was the last straw. I decided to end my silence. What I came to tell you is that a lawsuit is being filed against you for converting these two illiterate, ignorant women without their husbands' consent. The case will come up before a white magistrate soon. Let's see how fair white man's justice is.

SUNDARDAS *stands up.*

SUNDARDAS: Goodbye. (*Turns to* RADHU DAS.) Are you coming with me? Don't spend a minute longer here. All they're interested in is your conversion.

RADHU DAS *does not budge.* SUTTON *and* LACEY *look at each other in surprise. Exit* SUNDARDAS.

Scene II

LACEY'*s drawing room. Afternoon.* MARUA *and* BALABHADRA *are doing up the table.*

MARUA: You know something, David? I think I'll convert, after all.

BALABHADRA: What does it matter whether you do or don't. After all, you're just a maid servant in a house belonging to Christians. You live under their roof and share their food. You've been ostracised already, you've been thrown out of your caste.

MARUA: How come these padres, who are always begging people to become Christians, have never asked me to convert?

BALABHADRA: Look, you're a woman and a maid besides. Not exactly a prize catch, are you? What glory would there be for the padres if they got you to convert? Or take me. I've lost my caste, my home, my village. So why should they bother about me? But Marua, all this is to our advantage, if you ask me. We remain as much Hindu as Christian—call us by whatever name you please, thank you; it makes no difference to us.

MARUA: Have you misplaced the forks? Not again!

BALABHADRA: (*Looking for them.*) Oh, the damn forks! Now, now, where could I have put them? You know something, Mary? Let them crack their crazy heads over religion and conversion; to us what matters is laying the table, arranging the cutlery and stuff like that.

MARUA: You couldn't be more right, David, my boy. Baba Sundardas or Padre Lacey—there's no difference.

Enter LACEY *and* SUTTON.

LACEY: I knew the verdict would go against us. I've known it ever since the case came up in the court of the collector of the pilgrim tax.

SUTTON: The only silver lining—if it can be called that—is that Sundardas got a chance to heap praise on English justice.

LACEY: English justice—ha! The husbands were allowed to strip every bit of jewellery off their wives in the open courtroom. The poor women had to give back their clothes too. The child was plucked from Kamali's breast and handed to the father. The husbands declared their wives to be dead and that they'd observe the funeral rites for them. Is that English justice?

SUTTON: How hard the magistrate tried to implicate us!

LACEY: Maybe he wasn't able to, but he did direct us to sign fifty-rupee bonds ensuring that henceforth we would refrain from converting married women without their husbands' consent. And he ordered copies of his directive to be sent to all the missions and preachers.

SUTTON: An unfair decision, a most unfair decision. I'm going to petition to the governor general against it. (*Pauses thoughtfully.*) But what good will that do? We've already written to the governor general several times about the Jagannath temple. The other day Gangadhar signed and sent a petition that all monetary support to the temple must stop immediately, but as usual there's been no reply. I don't suppose there will be one.

LACEY: This verdict will hit us hard. We've already lost some of the natives' esteem; their respect for us has taken a beating.

SUTTON: The worst thing is that they no longer fear us at all. If a Hindu holy man can drag us into the court and get us fined, won't that lead them to increase their efforts to disrupt our meetings and preaching?

LACEY: The Calcutta Herald has asked us for information on the case.

SUTTON: We'll send them a complete report, showing out how the Company's laws and officials are ranged against the missionaries.

LACEY: Brother Bampton had sent word that he would be present in the courtroom when the verdict was rendered, but he wasn't there. It would have been useful to discuss the case with him.

SUTTON: Brother Bampton is very sick; I wonder if he'll ever be able to leave Puri again.

LACEY: He should go back to England, for his own health; but he won't even think of it.

SUTTON: As long as his greatest desire remains unfulfilled, to make a Christian out of at least one native of Puri.

LACEY: God willing he might yet succeed.

SUTTON: What does it matter if he hasn't been able to convert a single Hindu, his achievements are truly impressive. It was he who stood in front of the Great Temple and preached to the priests; it was he who entered the pagoda at Konark and spread the word of Christ. Really, it took someone like Brother Bampton to stick it out in Puri against overwhelming odds.

LACEY: Puri is indeed our testing ground.

SUTTON: I know, I know. My Charlotte died within a month of arriving there. Whenever I visit her grave I cannot help but curse that place as the vilest on earth.

LACEY: On a sad occasion like today I'm reminded of the day I left Serampore for Orissa. Dr. Carey said to me: Brother Lacey, I can't pray for you in the open congregation, but I will give you three pieces of advice. One, it is your duty to preach the Gospel of our Lord; two, God has said His words will come true; and three, He will remove all obstacles when He deems fit.

SUTTON: Praise to the Lord.

From outside the sounds of a palanquin being lowered to the ground. Enter an ailing BAMPTON, *barely able to walk. He makes for the nearest chair and sinks onto it, catching his breath.*

LACEY: Brother Bampton, we had given up hope.

BAMPTON: (*With considerable difficulty.*) Sorry, I couldn't make it to the courtroom.

SUTTON: Have you heard the verdict?

BAMPTON: Yes, but I'm not disheartened. We'll have to persevere despite disappointments, obstacles and enemies.

LACEY: Brother Bampton, you're an extraordinary person.

BAMPTON: I once thought so myself, but I began to cave in when

I contracted tuberculosis three years ago. My health went to pieces. I went to Calcutta for a change of air, but that did little good. I even took long spells by the sea, but nothing helped. I'm only forty-three, but I feel like an old man of eighty or more. I used to love riding, but now I find it a torture. The palanquin is about the only form of transportation I can stand. It drains me so much to stand that I'm forced to sit on a chair when I preach. Still, none of this matters, and happily shall I go to our Lord when the call comes. The only thing which saddens me is what will become of the poor native heathens of Orissa!

Enter GANGADHAR *and* RADHU DAS. *After exchanging greetings, they take their seats.*

LACEY: Gangadhar, have you heard the verdict?
GANGADHAR: Yes.
RADHU DAS: That seems to be the only topic of discussion in the town.
GANGADHAR: Did Sundara Baba come to see you?
SUTTON: Have you been to his ashram?
GANGADHAR: I was there a few days ago. Sundara Baba said he'd come to Cuttack to meet you the day the Court rendered its judgement.
LACEY: What else did he say?
GANGADHAR: He abused and threatened me, much the same way as he abused and threatened Ramachandra and Krupasindhu after their conversion. Sundara Baba has changed a lot.
RADHU DAS: People are talking against him.
LACEY: What!
GANGADHAR: They're saying that Sundara Baba is sinning with his women disciples, that he's secretly indulging in idol worship.
SUTTON: To tell you frankly, I've never really been able to trust a Hindu holy man. No Hindu holy man is up to any good. In my book of grammar there's an example which I think fits a Hindu holy man to a T:

Ignorant and foolish as a rule
Pretending to be holy out of greed;
To amass wealth
He roams the countryside
For more and more disciples;
Shorn of wisdom and piety
But acting as high and mighty;
He's a cheat, a turncoat, a bandit,
A fake, a sham, a dacoit;
He lives by his wiles;
Holy ashes, loin clothes, matted hair
Sleight of hand tricks passed off as miracles.

Sundara Baba is one such holy man; no better than the other charlatans.

GANGADHAR: I think he has gone mad.

LACEY: Not mad, but bad. How dare he file a suit against us, drag us to Court and have us fined!

SUTTON: We should have no relations with him. Gangadhar, stop visiting his ashram.

Enter SUNDARDAS *with a few disciples.*

SUNDARDAS: I beg your pardon for arriving without an invitation.

LACEY: (*Angrily.*) Just why are you here? We want nothing to do with you.

SUNDARDAS: Calm down, Brother Lacey, calm down. (*Turns to his disciples.*) Sit down, children. (*The disciples make themselves comfortable on the floor.*) All the padres are present—William Bampton, Charles Lacey, Amos Sutton, Gangadhar Sarangi. And the convert Radhu Das as well. Good. Good. I might as well say what I came to say.

LACEY: We want nothing to do with you any more.

SUNDARDAS: Patience, Brother Lacey, patience. Give me a hearing first. I'm going to tell you about Jesus Christ the Saviour. Jesus himself was like a child. And you know what he said about children, don't you? Suffer the little children to come unto me, and forbid them not: for of such is the kingdom of God. A child like this was Krishna. They are the same—Krishna and Jesus Christ. One and the same.

BAMPTON: (*Angry, excited.*) Blasphemy!

SUNDARDAS: (*Brushing him aside.*) Let me explain. Krishna was born in the Jadu community; Jesus was born a Jew. Both were born into families that tended animals; both had to be shielded from royal vengeance; both Mary and Devaki had immaculate conceptions. Krishna was smuggled away to Gopapur for fear of Kamsa, Jesus to Syria for fear of Herod. Both Kamsa and Herod were notorious for infanticide. Both Krishna and Jesus were long-armed, with glowing complexions. With a single grain of food Krishna once fed twelve thousand Brahmins in the Kamyak forest; Jesus fed five thousand people with five loaves of bread and two fishes. Christ walked on water, Krishna underneath it. Krishna turned stone to butter, Christ turned water to wine. Each was hailed as god. Both straightened the humps of hump-backs. Krishna had twelve cowherd friends, Christ twelve apostles.

SUTTON: What nonsense! The Bible says: Beware of false prophets, which come to you in sheep's clothing, but inwardly they are ravening wolves.

LACEY: Then if any man shall say unto you, Lo, here is Christ, or there; believe it not. For there shall arise false Christs, and false prophets, and shall shew great signs and wonders; insomuch that, if it were possible, they shall deceive the very elect.

BAMPTON: (*Rising to his feet with difficulty.*) Sundardas is guilty of blasphemy.

SUNDARDAS: Padre Bampton, you are a sick man. I will heal you with a miracle. Jesus Christ gave sight to the blind, speech to the mute, hearing to the deaf and life to the dead.

BAMPTON: In your Hindu religion the gods and goddesses killed, but our Jesus Christ brought the dead back to life.

SUNDARDAS: Good, good. I too will bring new life to the people. In Kaliyug I'm Jesus Christ. The gospel is what I preach. I have twelve disciples. (*Counts on his fingers.*) Daitari Nayak, Ganga Mohanty, Krupasindhu Sahu, Sudarshan Rout, Parameswar Malla, Purushottam Mohapatra, Bamdev Sahu, Parsuram Rout, Hari Padhi, Ramachandra Jachak, Gangadhar Sarangi. That makes eleven. (*He walks up to* RADHU DAS *and fondles his chin.*) And Radhu Das, my Judas Iscariot.

BAMPTON: (*Jumping about.*) Blasphemy! Blasphemy! (*Recites to himself.*) And as he sat upon the mount of Olives, the disciples came unto him privately, saying, Tell us, when shall these things be? And what shall be the sign of thy coming, and of the end of the world? And Jesus answered and said unto them, Take heed that no man deceive you. For many shall come in my name, saying, I am Christ; and shall deceive many. (*Pause.*) Sundardas is a false prophet. He is trying to pull the wool over your eyes.

SUNDARDAS: (*Brushing him aside.*) Did you understand what I said, my children? I am Krishna, I am Jesus Christ.

LACEY: Please leave now.

SUNDARDAS: (*Rattles off like a madman.*) I will, but I'll take my disciples with me. No, on second thought, let them remain here to preach my Commandments, the Commandments of Jesus Christ. I'll only take my old servant Radhu Das with me.

LACEY: If you don't leave, you'll be thrown out.

SUNDARDAS: I'll take Radhu Das with me.

RADHU DAS: But I don't want to go with you.

SUNDARDAS: What? What did you say, Radhu Das? You've become smart, I see! Don't you know Sundardas, Radhu Judas Iscariot Das? Of course you'll come with me. If not today, then some other day, but come you will. And if I ever hear that you've become a Christian, I'll give you a bone-breaking beating, much worse than what you got at the hands of the villagers of Bhairavpur. Better keep that in mind. (*Looks around.*) All right, my children. Let's go. Goodbye, Padre Lacey, goodbye Padre Sutton. (*Walks up to* BAMPTON.) Goodbye Padre Bampton.

Exit SUNDARDAS *with his disciples. Silence.*

LACEY: We should file a police complaint.

SUTTON: Patience, Brother Lacey, there's no point in getting worked up. We must be watchful, Sundardas is our enemy now. He has openly insulted us. True, we must do something about it, but we must be careful.

BAMPTON: (*Getting up in agitation.*) Beware of false prophets, which come to you in sheep's clothing, but inwardly they are ravening wolves.

BAMPTON *crashes to the floor. The others rush to pick him up.*

SUTTON: Brother Bampton!

LACEY: Brother Bampton!

Scene III

Same as the last scene: LACEY'*s drawing room. Morning.* SUTTON *and* LACEY *are seated. Behind them,* ANN, MARUA *and* BALABHADRA *are busy laying the table.*

LACEY: Already two more years have gone by. How quickly time passes. Nine years already since I came to Orissa.

SUTTON: Sometimes I feel gratified about our achievement, while at other times I'm racked by a sense of failure.

LACEY: When I left England, my friends told me I was a fool if I thought I would convert even a single soul in Orissa. They were sure no worshipper of Jagannath would ever take to Christianity. But my faith in my mission remained unshaken; I knew I'd succeed someday. And it's only six years since we started our Mission here and already our efforts have borne fruit. And what a catch to start with—a self-respecting, blue-blooded Brahmin, well-versed in the scriptures!

SUTTON: Gangadhar is a big support to us. He lost his home, his land and family by becoming a Christian.

LACEY: Thank God we were able to buy that land next to the chapel. Now we can build him a house.

SUTTON: I never thought that piece of land would be ours. But right from the beginning Radhu Das was confident that the owner could be persuaded to sell it.

LACEY: I'm sure he'd have sold the Hanuman idol for a price too. We could have had it broken into pieces publicly so that people would have realised that stones have no supernatural powers. (*Pause.*) But Brother Sutton, why do you sometimes feel that we've achieved nothing in Orissa?

SUTTON: When I first came here I had grandiose hopes that the entire population would convert in no time. But what have we accomplished? We've converted only a handful. We've built a chapel on the ruins of a temple. We've fallen so short of our dreams! The dreams of an Orissa with all its beautiful Hindu temples razed to the ground! The Jagannath Temple at Puri continues to reign over the land; the Hindus have not given up idol worship, or the caste system. We still visit fairs and bazaars and preach our mouths dry, but Brother Lacey, to what avail?

LACEY: Brother Sutton, you give in to despair too easily. Take your own example. You compiled and published an Oriya Grammar—the first of its kind in the language. Just think what a help it is to the learners, and to the language itself.

SUTTON: Are you under the illusion that the Oriya language is—or ever was—in need of my grammar book, Brother Lacey? I worked on the book because I thought it would help us missionaries. If you take a dispassionate view, what have we really done here other than preach?

LACEY: But the rest is the Company's business.

SUTTON: The Company's business! Does it have any aim other than making money? It did not hesitate to come to an understanding with the priests of Jagannath temple simply to reduce its administrative problems.

Enter the VILLAGERS. *They look at the padres who nod genially at them.*

LACEY: Welcome! Welcome!

VILLAGER I: We were passing by and thought of looking up the old padre who used to come to our village to preach, the one who used to ride a horse. We haven't seen him around for a long time.

SUTTON: That's Brother Bampton, he passed away two years ago. May his soul rest in peace.

VILLAGER II: Dead? He was a good man, the old padre was. Never harmed anyone, not even a fly; never lost his temper, no matter how much he was ridiculed.

LACEY: Brother Sutton here and I are padres like the late lamented Brother Bampton. Please sit down. I will give you copies of the Book and explain the message of our Lord Jesus Christ to you.

VILLAGER III: We don't need your books and printed papers; we just wanted to look up the lovable old padre. We want nothing to do with Christians.

VILLAGER I: Did the old padre have a family?

LACEY: A wife and two sons. They went back to England after his death.

SUTTON: Brother Bampton was laid to rest at Puri; you can visit his grave if you wish.

VILLAGER I: What an idea! We can't even make it to Puri to worship our own Lord Jagannath. Visit padre Bampton's grave indeed! He was a nice soul though.

Exit the VILLAGERS, *talking among themselves.*

SUTTON: For as long as I lived in Puri after Brother Bampton's death I never forgot to put some flowers on his grave every time I visited Charlotte's.

LACEY: Brother Bampton was dear to God and He took him back early. Jesus must have complimented him: Well done, my good and faithful servant! Bampton must have run into Charlotte in heaven.

SUTTON: Such a wonderful man, but what an awful time he had at the end. He was completely mad. The day he died he recited from the Bible: O Lord, rebuke me not in thy wrath: neither chasten me in thy hot displeasure. Foe thine arrows stick fast in me, and thy hand presseth me sore.

LACEY: One regret I will always have is that I didn't see him before he died. It wasn't Sister Bampton's fault, she sent word in time but I started out late. By the time I reached Puri his body had already been nailed inside the coffin. He was buried next to Charlotte.

SUTTON: The doctor at Puri told me about Brother Bampton's last moments. It seems a nurse asked him: 'How do you feel?' and Brother Bampton replied: 'Wonderful, I'm on my way to heaven.' Sister Bampton was holding his head in her lap and she whispered into his ear: 'Yes, my dear, you're going to heaven.' 'That's right,' murmured Bampton. Those were his last words.

LACEY: Who knows what he was thinking about in those last moments! I remember it like yesterday the first time I met him in Puri. Always eager to jump on his horse and gallop off to preach. Perhaps his last thoughts were: Bring me my horse, I'm on my way to heaven!

SUTTON: We've lost many friends in Orissa—Brother Pegg's three young daughters, my wife and five-month-old son, Brother Joshua Cropper and Brother Bampton. And think of the misfortunes that have visited the land in the meantime—first the floods in Balasore, and then the Great Famine, which ravaged the entire land. We had to close down the Mission in Puri on two occasions. This time it has fallen to my lot to do so yet again.

LACEY: I'm sure you will soon regain your health and return to Puri.

SUTTON: Who knows! I'm not so hopeful. My health seems to worsen by the day. I think I need a long break; perhaps I'll go to the Americas for a spell. Who knows when I'll return!

LACEY: Brother Sutton, you'll be all right soon. We owe Orissa a lot, and there's a lot more to do here.

SUTTON: What more can we do? Maybe convert a few more people, that's about all.

LACEY: We were betrayed by the person we had hoped would become the first Christian of the land.

SUTTON: So what if Sundardas has not become a Christian? Look at all his disciples and devotees—Gangadhar Sarangi, Ramachandra Jachak, Krupasindhu Sahu, Kamali and Daani, Daitari Nayak, Karuna Sahu, Kishu Padhy, Hari Padhy, Trilochan, Bamdev, Balaram and all. They've all become Christians.

LACEY: You're forgetting Radhu Das.

SUTTON: Right. But what a pity that Sundardas, whom we expected to help us preach and proselytize, has become our greatest enemy and obstacle!

LACEY: He's become a false messiah; he's gone mad.

SUTTON: Sometimes I wonder whether we drove him mad. His madness seemed to become complete after we converted Radhu Das.

LACEY: He roughed up Radhu Das.

SUTTON: We filed a case against him and had him sent to jail. Earlier, he had won his case and had us sign a bond. Now we're even.

LACEY: The verdict was fair. Sundardas himself was full of praise for it.

SUTTON: Last time we denounced the same magistrate because his verdict was against us. This time we were pleased with him because it was in our favour.

LACEY: Nevertheless, Sundardas wasn't right to beat up Radhu Das. Radhu converted voluntarily; nobody forced him.

SUTTON: Sometimes I wonder what the poor converts have gotten in life? By becoming Christians they simply traded this life for an afterlife; they lost everything here on earth.

LACEY: What are you saying, Brother Sutton? We saved lost souls; we saved sinners.

SUTTON: They lost their homes, their families broke up—husbands were separated from wives, children from parents. Villages went up in flames; discord and strife became the ruling passions; peace was destroyed. Wouldn't they have been better off without us?

LACEY: Brother Sutton, you need to rest; you aren't well.

SUTTON: Brother Lacey, I'm fine. Please don't worry about me.

LACEY: It's not as if we've confined ourselves only to preaching and proselytizing. We've done a good deal for these people—set up schools and hospitals, controlled epidemics. We've put an end to many an evil practice in the Jagannath temple; we've put an end to human sacrifices by the hill people.

SUTTON: What would have happened if we hadn't come here?

LACEY: The natives would have remained sunk in the mire of sin, ignorance and darkness.

SUTTON: Are they pleased that we're here?

LACEY: Why not? (*He calls out to* MARUA *and others.*) Mary, David, Radhu Das. Come here please. (*They approach him.*) What do you have to say about it? Are you people pleased? Mary, you were ostracized by your people in the village and they looked down upon you, but here you got a chance for a decent life—good clothes, good food. And you David, you were born in a little hell-hole. Your father sold you to the Kondhs, who wanted to sacrifice you, but here you are looked after and given an education too. You Radhu Das, you ran after false saints like Sundardas and others for years, wanting but not getting the enlightenment you sought, and which you found here. What do you have to say, Mary, David and Radhu Das? Aren't I right?

They nod their heads in agreement.

SUTTON: Answer me, Marua, Balabhadra and Radhu Das: is this the life you wanted? Have you found peace and happiness?

They remain silent. Enter SUNDARDAS. *Everyone is amazed.* SUNDARDAS *has an unruly beard. He is glum, no longer his smiling, sprite self. He proceeds to shake hands with everyone.*

SUNDARDAS: Are you surprised to see me?

LACEY: We certainly didn't expect you.

SUTTON: Please take a chair. You're welcome here.

SUNDARDAS: (*Takes a chair.*) I got out of the jail this morning.

They let me out a little earlier for good behaviour. I thought I would come and thank you before I returned to Kujibar.

LACEY: Thank us?

SUNDARDAS: For having me sent to jail.

LACEY: It was Radhu Das who filed the case against you. You assaulted him.

SUNDARDAS: You know nothing about my relationship with Radhu Das, then. He was used to being roughed up once in a while, and he didn't mind it. No, padre, the case was not between him and me. Remember Kamali and Daani? Their case wasn't filed by me but by their husbands, though the war was actually between you and me. We fought it through them; they were mere pawns. Radhu Das wasn't my opponent, nor were the husbands of Kamali and Daani yours. The opponents were you and I.

LACEY: But you put obstacles in our path; you fell out with your disciples when they embraced Christianity. You made yourself our opponent.

SUNDARDAS: But there was a time when you looked upon me as a friend, remember? You complimented me, congratulated me when I preached your Ten Commandments. But when . . .

LACEY: (*Interrupting him.*) You pretended to be Jesus Christ.

SUTTON: Brother Lacey, let him speak.

SUNDARDAS: Brother Sutton, there's a reason why I want to thank him for the jail term. People normally consider the faraway Himalayas or an ashram inside the deepest forest as the ideal place for meditation and reflection, but I think prison is just as good a place, if not better. Not only are you alone, but your ego, your inflated notions about yourself, take a battering. And that is the first step toward true meditation.

SUNDARDAS *falls silent, immersed in his thoughts.*

SUTTON: You were telling us about your prison experience.

SUNDARDAS: Oh yes, I was telling you about what I came to realize. I had all the time in the world to contemplate: who I am, what I want, what I have become? When I was the commander of the Athgarh army I was equally happy—I loved big game hunting, for one thing—but one day I decided to change the course of my life.

SUTTON: That's because you wanted a better life.

SUNDARDAS: I don't know what I wanted, I really don't. What made me want to change was the sudden realisation that the life I had lived until then was all wrong, a big mistake; that all I had achieved or done was insignificant, meaningless. (*Pause.*) I began to analyse my past and wanted my future to be different. That's how I began to study the scriptures, discuss them with monks and sadhus before I shut myself in Kujibar ashram to meditate. The long meditation led me to certain ideas about life, society, ethics and morality.

SUTTON: The Kujibar ashram was your creation.

SUNDARDAS: I had no thought of establishing an ashram. But so deep is people's respect for sadhus and sanyasis that they build an ashram wherever these monks stop even for a while. So before I knew what was happening I found an ashram built and some people declaring themselves to be my disciples. Lo and behold, overnight I came to be known as Sundara Baba.

LACEY: Hindu society is teeming with false saints and sadhus; many ashrams are dens of iniquity.

SUNDARDAS: Other religions have had their fair share of such creatures and institutions too. Name one for which wars haven't been fought, and which hasn't sown the seeds of discord and strife? Anyway, I wasn't telling about that, just about my experience.

SUTTON: Please go on. You were saying that one day you decided to change your life.

SUNDARDAS: I came to understand what constitutes an ideal life. But was it easy to practice? Society makes many demands. I wanted a simple life as ordinary Sundardas, but I was saddled with being Sadhu Sundardas. From a seeker, a trier, I became a realised soul, a sadhu, and the head of an ashram on top of all that. There was no longer any possibility of living life on my own terms. And

I found the life heading an ashram no less stifling than life as an army commander. The moment you cease to live life according to your own notions, and try to live up to other people's expectations, life becomes painful. Once I was identified as a Baba and tied to an ashram, the place began to bustle with visitors and I began to give speeches, to start teaching, and preaching. Some welcomed it, many denounced it; some became disciples. I began to make efforts to get more and more people to turn to my teachings.

SUTTON: There's nothing wrong in preaching universal, eternal values.

SUNDARDAS: A truly realised soul should be more concerned with living a good life himself. But I was taken up with my increasing desire to propagate my views and gain more and more followers. Practices like idol worship and the caste system run so deep in our society that it wasn't possible for me to demolish them. When my persuasion, my reasoning and arguments all failed, I took to working miracles to instil fear and faith into people's minds. A man who will believe that a flower can be plucked out of air will swallow anything.

LACEY: Saints can work miracles.

SUNDARDAS: My disciples deified me as a miracle-working saint. Krupasindhu and his wife Devaki had lost many children, but after they joined the ashram not one but three of their children survived; all that was attributed to my powers. But when one of Kamali's children died it was not held against me. I was covered by the cloak of false sainthood.

SUTTON: But your teachings were sound.

SUNDARDAS: One must practice what one teaches. For example, I preached against anger but on many an occasion I couldn't curb my own.

SUTTON: No man is perfect; everyone has some weakness.

SUNDARDAS: It's not just a matter of weakness. Far from it. I think I never believed in what I professed. Marua hit the nail on the head when she accused me of discriminating between men and women. In my ashram I always claimed to consider men and women as equals, but I couldn't bring myself to treat Gangadhar's conversion without his wife's consent the same as Kamali's without her husband's. In fact, there was no difference between the two. This morning when I got out of jail, I found a few disciples waiting. They thought I'd start preaching again. But I thought no, I must first practise what I wish to preach. So I avoided them and came here to see you.

SUNDARDAS *falls silent as if he has nothing else to add.*

SUTTON: You were telling us about your relationship with us.

SUNDARDAS: Oh yes, I became acquainted with your scriptures much before I met any of you. The first book I came across was the Ten Commandments. Until then I didn't know about the Bible or Jesus Christ. I took to the Commandments immediately—not because they came directly from your god or because they were a part of your Holy Bible but because they seemed to me the basic tenets, the essence of all religion. Later when I read about Jesus Christ I began to grow to love and respect him.

LACEY: But you turned against us!

SUNDARDAS: You did not ask me to preach the Ten Commandments; I did that on my own. You did not ask me for my disciples; I gave them to you. But you misunderstood.

LACEY: We wanted you to convert, to accept our faith.

SUNDARDAS: You wanted me to become a Christian. But why should I give up my religion and embrace yours? Nothing prevents me from practising or preaching what I think is right. Nothing is imposed on me. I didn't believe in idol worship or in many other Hindu rituals, or in the caste system. The priests and the Brahmins hated the sight of me, but that didn't matter. I preached only to those who would come to me. People were free to accept or reject my teachings. The trouble started when I sent my disciples out to preach your Ten Commandments.

SUTTON: But don't you think the Ten Commandments should be widely preached? Don't they represent the true religion?

SUNDARDAS: Human life is more important than religion. If missionary activity creates dissension, what's the use of it?

SUTTON: Every religion wants to increase the number of believers.

SUNDARDAS: I had enough time in the jail to think about all that. Anything that complicates the human situation can't be true faith. Faith is personal; and every man should preserve it within his heart, his home. Those are the true places of worship—those are his temples, his mosques, his churches. Once you put it out in the open, in the bazaar, on the street, in the court room, there'll be nothing but bad blood, strife and division.

Silence.

SUNDARDAS: I'm sorry I've been doing all the talking. Tell me about yourselves, Brother Lacey, Brother Sutton.

SUTTON: I will be leaving Orissa shortly.

SUNDARDAS: That's a sensible decision, Brother Sutton. You look ill, and need a change of air. God bless you and keep you well.

LACEY: Will you have some tea?

SUNDARDAS: (*Rising to his feet.*) No thank you. Some other time perhaps.

SUNDARDAS *shakes hand with them.*

SUNDARDAS: God bless you all. Now, my children, Radhu there, and you Marua and Balabhadra, how long do you want to live as exiles? Come along, come home with me.

Exit SUNDARDAS.
After a moment of hesitation RADHU, MARUA and BALABHADRA *follow. A tired* LACEY *helps* SUTTON *to a chair and flops down into another.*

Author's Note

Sundardas (1720?-1883) is one of the lesser known sadhus of India; he is little known even in Orissa where he lived and preached. His early life is shrouded in mystery, but we get a wealth of information about his later life from the journals and books by Baptist missionaries.

Orissa was occupied by the British in 1803. Since trade was its main objective, the East India Company did not want to antagonise the local population and so kept good relationship with the Puri temple and its priests. It is for this reason that missionaries were not allowed into its territories till 1922.

Sundardas of Kujibar Ashram (in Chowdwar, Cuttack) was an unusual sadhu; he had forsaken many of the practices connected with traditional Hindu monasteries—idol worship, caste discrimination, exclusion of women and so on. It was, therefore, no surprise that he accepted many Christian precepts from the religious tracts which the missionaries were then distributing. Sundardas came into personal contact with the missionaries in 1922.

The first meeting of Sundardas with the missionaries and what followed were rather dramatic and the play is based on these real events and personalities. Missionaries Bampton, Lacey and Sutton are as much historical as are Sundardas and his followers Gangadhar Sarangi, Ramchandra Jachak and others. The story of the confrontation between the sadhu and the missionaries and their strange relationship are based on historical records; the play uses many of their dialogues verbatim as they appear in the writings of that time. The following is the chronology of events (for which specific dates are available) dealt with in the play:

1822 February: William Bampton arrives in Orissa and sets up the Orissa Baptist Mission.

1823 December: Charles Lacey arrives in Orissa.
1825 March: Amos Sutton joins Charles Lacey.
1826 January: Sundardas reads the Christian tracts for the first time.
1826 November: The first chapel opens at Cuttack.
1827 November: Sundardas sends the padres his letter from Kujibar.
1827 December: William Bampton makes his first convert—Irun Senapati of Berhampur.
1828 March: Gangadhar Sarangi converts.
1829 November: Ramachandra Jachak converts.
1830 April: Krupasindhu Sahu converts.
1830 December: William Bampton passes away in Puri.
1832 July: Radhu Das converts.
1833 January: Amos Sutton leaves Orissa.

The following quotes from the Bible (King James version) have been used in the play:

Act I

Scene I

P. 21 (Gangadhar) Exodus 21: 16
P. 23 (Gangadhar) Isaiah 11: 6-8

Scene II

P. 35 (Lacey) Matthew 5: 10-11

Act II

Scene I

P. 38 (Lacey) Matthew 6: 9-13
Luke 11: 2
P. 39 (Gangadhar) Exodus 20: 3-5
P. 39-40 (Lacey) Psalms 115: 4-8

Scene II

P. 44 (Bampton) Peter 5: 6-11
P. 44 (Bampton) John 3: 16

Scene III

P. 46 (Villager II) Exodus 20: 7
P. 48 (Sutton) Roman 1: 22-25

Act III

Scene I

P. 68 (Lacey) Isaiah 35: 1-2
P. 71 (Lacey) Matthew 1: 18
P. 73 (Bampton) Mathew 28: 18-20

Scene II

P. 85 (Sundardas) Mark 10:14
P. 85 (Sutton) Matthew 7: 15
P. 85 (Lacey) Matthew 24: 23-24
P. 86 (Bampton) Matthew 24: 3-5
P. 87 (Bampton) Matthew 7: 15

Scene III

P. 90 (Sutton) Psalm 38

A selected Bibliography is enclosed for those interested in knowing more on the subject.

Selected Bibliography

1. *A Narrative of the Mission to Orissa* (Supported by the New Connexion of General Baptists in England, 1833) with an introductory essay by J. C. Ewing. Glasgow, 1934.
2. *Baptismal Covenant.* The Baptist Mission Press, 1837.
3. *Calcutta Christian Observer.* Journal. Calcutta (1833-1865).
4. *Calcutta Missionary Herald.* Journal. Calcutta (1840-1860).
5. Carey S. Pearce. *Dawn on the Kond Hills.* London, 1936.
6. Laurie, W. F. B. *Orissa: The Garden of Superstitions and Idolatry,* with an Account of the British Connection with the Temple of Jagannath. Edinburgh, 1850.
7. Lovett, R. *The History of London Missionary Society, 1795-1895.*
8. Myers, John Brown. *Centenary Volume of the Baptist Missionary Society,* London (1792-1892).
9. Pati, Ratnakar. *Mahatma Sadhu Sundardas's Advaitism or Absolute Brahmo.* Cuttack, 1950.
10. Patra, Prafulla Kumar. *Orissare Baptist Missionary Society-ra Karya Evam Khristiya Mandali Stapanara Itihasa* (Oriya), Cuttack, 1943.
11. Peggs, James. (i) *Pilgrim Tax in India: Facts and Observations.* London, 1830 (ii) *India's Cries to British Humanity.* London, 1832 (iii) *A History of the general Baptists Mission.* London, 1846.
12. Sahu, Dr. Krishna Mohan. *Mahatma Sadhu Sundardas* (Oriya). Cuttack, 1948.
13. *Selections from the Records of the Government of India* (Home Department) *No. V* (History of the Rise and Progress of the Operations for the Suppression of Human Sacrifice and Female Infanticide in the Hill Tracts of Orissa). F. Carberry, Bengal Military Orphan Press. Calcutta, 1854.
14. Singh, Rev. Jayanand. *Orissare Khrista-Dharmodaya O Keteka Adya Khristiananka Jibani* (Oriya). Cuttack, 1914 (Second Edition, 1985).
15. Sutton, Amos. (i) *Orissa and its Evangelisation* (Interspersed with suggestions respecting the more efficient conducting of Indian Missions). Calcutta, 1850 (ii) *A Narrative of the Mission to Orissa.* Boston, 1833 (iii) *An Introductory Grammar of the Oriya Language.* Calcutta, 1831.
16. Young, Rev. *Biography of Indian Christians.* 1892.

Note on the Author and Translators

Dr. Jagannath Prasad Das (b. 1936) is an eminent Oriya poet, playwright and fiction writer. He is also an art historian with several volumes on Orissan art to his credit. His books have been widely translated into Hindi, English and other Indian languages, and his plays have been performed in many languages in different parts of India. He left the Indian Administrative Service to devote himself to full time research and creative writing. He lives and works in Delhi.

Paul St-Pierre, Professor of Linguistics & Translation Studies at the University of Montreal, has collaborated on various translations from Oriya into English, including the translation of the first Oriya play (*The Holy Man: A Play,* Sateertha Publications) and of the first Oriya novel (Fakir Mohan Senapati's *Six Acres and a Third,* to be published by University of California Press and Penguin India). He is currently working (with **Leelawati Mohapatra** and **K K Mohapatra**) on an anthology of modern Oriya short stories. The Mohapatras have previously edited (with Sudhansu Mohanty) *The HarperCollins Book of Oriya Short Stories* (HarperCollins, 1998).